THE HANDBOOK for *Being Human*

A Soothing Guide To Calm The Chaos
In Your Spiritual Awakening

Aida Jasmine

The Handbook for Being Human: A Soothing Guide To Calm The Chaos In Your Spiritual Awakening © Aida Jasmine 2024

www.soulfinity.com.au

The moral rights of Aida Jasmine to be identified as the author of this work have been asserted in accordance with the Copyright Act 1968.

First published in Australia 2024

ISBN 978-0-6486287-0-5

Any opinions expressed in this work are exclusively those of the author and are not necessarily the views held or endorsed by the publisher.

All rights reserved. No part of this publication may be reproduced or transmitted by any means, electronic, photocopying or otherwise, without prior written permission of the author.

Disclaimer

All the information, techniques, skills and concepts contained within this publication are of the nature of general comment only, and are not in any way recommended as individual advice. The intent is to offer a variety of information to provide a wider range of choices now and in the future, recognising that we all have widely diverse circumstances and viewpoints. Should any reader choose to make use of the information herein, this is their decision, and the author and publisher/s do not assume any responsibilities whatsoever under any conditions or circumstances. The author does not take responsibility for the business, financial, personal or other success, results or fulfilment upon the readers' decision to use this information. It is recommended that the reader obtain their own independent advice.

Mumma. Thank you for your undying support and belief in me. Your strength will continue to support me through my days.

To all spiritual beings exploring this incredible human experience, may this handbook help you to calm the chaos through your spiritual awakening and support you through life.

This book is dedicated to you.

Foreword

I have the pleasure of knowing Aida, the author and Divine channel of this handbook for life, and I also have the pleasure of being her Divine counterpart. You may think this makes me biased in my opinion of her; however, I am honoured that Aida feels safe enough to entrust me writing the foreword for her first book as there will, no doubt, be many more.

I have seen first-hand how Aida lives and breathes every word that was written in this book on a daily basis. The level and accountability she holds herself to, which was also transmitted into the energy of this book, will certainly radiate out to you while you read through it and taking part in the *SacredPlay*.

Aida's Divine Goddess and Divine Witch energy will hold your hand, guide you, and hold you accountable, just as if she were there next to you as you read. The balance of dark and light, of which Aida is fearless in living, creates the perfect balance for you to grow. There is no fluff here, only what is real for your human self and your spiritual self. Aida lives her passion, her power, her Goddess, her human, her everything, unashamedly, every day. She has done the work and continues to do the work included in this guide.

Aida has been a Divine guide her whole life, and it is an amazing gift that she now shares that wisdom with you.

Welcome to the start of the most incredible journey of your life so far.

Roy Bristow, Merlin

Table Of Contents

Foreword vii

Welcome 1

1: Why Are You Here? 11

2: Remember Who You Are 27

3: Soul Alignment 41

4: Navigating The Different Dimensions 67

5: Developing Self-Mastery 73

6: The Four Interior Pillars 89

7: Living With Intention 105

8: The Universe Is Constantly Responding To You 111

9: Universal Laws And Spiritual Principles 129

10: Uncover Your Unique Soul Expression And Dharma ... 155

11: Attachment, Non-Attachment And Detachment 167

12: Your Intuition Is A Super Power 175

13: The Secret Power Of Decluttering 189

14: Spiritual By-Passing 205

15: The Transformative Power Of Forgiveness 211

16: Dark Night Of The Soul 219

17: The Gift Of Grief.. 227

18: Daily Rituals, Application, And Integration 243

The Beginning 249

Find Your Way Home 253

Gratitude 255

About Aida Jasmine 259

Welcome

Welcome, beloved. I feel blessed and honoured that you selected this book to be your guide on your personal and spiritual path. I believe there are no accidents in life and no coincidences. Everything happens for a reason, and everything leads us to this very point, this very moment, here and now.

There is only now, and what we do, or don't do, in this moment. That is the power of choice, and you have made a very important choice in selecting this book to be your guide along your spiritual journey. For that decision, I feel very blessed and deeply grateful.

I believe the Universe is always conspiring in our favour; we have simply forgotten this truth. Along our journey of life, we have forgotten who we truly are: an Infinite Spiritual Being, a child of the Cosmos, an important part of the epic creation of the Universe and beyond, but no less significant. You have chosen to come here, to arrive on this Earth and play out some very important experiences as part of your soul journey and expansion. What an incredible adventure you have embarked upon, and now, you have this to show you the way home.

No more aimlessly wandering through life. No more what-ifs, doubts, or buts, only soul expansion, acceptance, and mastery: a journey to be embraced, revered, and joyful. Yes, it's a time of joy, celebration, and abundance, in all its delicious forms. We only need to allow it in and I will show you the way through this glorious life.

How It Began

The concept for this book began, as do many of my projects, as a vision from Spirit.

I was driving to meet a friend for tea when suddenly I received this 'download'. The name of the book you are holding boomed in my ear and my spirit team then proceeded to list all the chapters I was to cover. I was like, "Seriously? Now! Whilst I'm driving?!" That's how Spirit works with me, and my Guides often have a sense of humour. The messages are sometimes delivered in the most inconvenient times: when I am mindfully going about my business, driving, in the shower, bathroom breaks – you get my drift. I pulled over, activated the voice memo recording on my phone, and recited my download.

This is not my first try at writing this book. A previous attempt of this book already exists, from which I have launched and taught several courses, including achieving a self-mastery program, a soul activation, mastery and embodiment course, Witch and Mystery Schools, plus so much more. My legacy and programs are all based on empowering people to live a life led by purpose and filled with abundance.

You see, I've been doing this 'work' for a while, lifetimes even. I have written page upon page of deep insights, personal revelations, premonitions, lessons, teachings, all corresponding to helping others find their light to live a blissful, abundant life.

While writing, there was a small part of me that I held back in fear, a deep-seated fear from decades, centuries, and yes, lifetimes of being persecuted, ridiculed, outcast, and even killed in past lives for sharing this knowledge – acts committed by those who would wish to keep this knowledge hidden. I knew I had to overcome this fear because my purpose is to empower others. The wisdom contained herein these pages is transformative, with the potential to alter your path – autocorrect, so to speak – and guide you back to your true soul essence and path if you allow it.

This book is my life's work, several lifetimes, in fact. I innately teach, and I have been sharing this knowledge with others as a spiritual guide, mentor and embodiment teacher. I am what you might consider a spiritual activator: my purpose is to remind you of your innate power, your purpose, while guiding you back within.

For me, recognising my fear – the base of it and seeing it for what it was – helped me realise it was time to navigate through the resistance and finally bring this book to life. It wasn't a straightforward journey. Spirit would again and again continue to deliver messages about me sharing this knowledge with others; I resisted. I kept thinking, who am I to share this knowledge? The resistance continued until I acknowledged this was my ego's attempt at keeping me small, hidden, quiet, and, in its mind, safe. You may also relate to that in some area of your life.

We have many amazing spiritual teachers on this planet, Reverend Michael Bernard Beckwith, Eckhart Tolle, Louise Hay, Doreen Virtue, Carolyn Myss, Deepak Chopra, and Wayne Dyer, to name a few. However, Spirit kept telling me I have my own work to do, to remind you that there is no greater teacher than your sacred self. You are your greatest teacher. Whilst others may guide you, it is still your journey, your human experience, and, ultimately, the buck stops with you. That can be scary.

I will share with you now that I will not hold back. Much of what I know up to this point, in continuing your spiritual journey, is embedded within this book and already within you. We are here to embrace life. I am here to empower you to develop such a love and passion for life that you greet each day with such a fervour that you leap out of bed, excited for the new day.

It was during a meditation that I received more epic messages from Spirit, and then things really began to change. I had written the outline of this book years before; however, it was during this time when it became very clear what this book was to be about. The world needed a guidebook on how to be human. Many try to escape or attempt to find an antidote for life. I suggest we don't need an antidote; we need a handbook on how to navigate the human experience with ease and grace.

I began writing this book over the Christmas break. I sat down, and the bulk of it flowed out over two full days of writing. Spirit guided me: I listened and took inspired action. It was completed within a week, incorporating all knowledge and wisdom that I have gathered, downloaded, and learned during my journey: it's all encapsulated in this book, and now it's time to share it with the world.

You Are Here

This is not just another book for you to read, put down, and move on to the next. Someone recently commented to me such behaviour was aptly called 'shelf development', rather than self-development: a bookshelf filled with wisdom yet to be embodied. This book has been created to be used as a resource with daily practices for you to play each day. Yes, I mean play. Life is meant to be fun, engaging, happy, and fulfilled. This book will be your 'play-book', your daily handbook, filled with valuable, stimulating, and thought-provoking insights, designed to ignite your mind, heart, body, and soul, and for you to find the answers within.

Parts of this book will guide you to discovering your blocks and challenges, uncovering the root cause of your pain, discomfort, and dis-ease. Then it will lead you to alchemise the resistance and move forward through your life with greater peace and harmony. I believe it to be possible.

Learning to understand our emotions, how they impact our human experience and navigate through them, enables us to live a more empowered and fulfilled life.

As mentioned earlier, I will not hold back. At times, it may feel very direct in the way I share this knowledge, and I make no apologies. This wisdom is too profound to hold back.

Your brilliance is too great to be hidden. You are here, on this Earth, for a reason, and you deserve to live an abundant, blissful life.

This handbook is a guide on how to navigate the human experience as a spiritual being in the modern world. You may even experience a spiritual awakening whilst reading it. This book is for anyone ready to transcend their life, to shift from mediocre to magnificent, no matter where you are on your spiritual journey. I personally received many more up-loads, downloads and internal shifts as I wrote it.

This book is a guide to self-mastery, even soul-mastery. A guide to help you calm the chaos that can ensue during a spiritual awakening.

All that you seek is inside of you. All your bliss, power, strength, courage, abundance, prosperity, happiness…all the deliciousness that life has to offer is already within you. My purpose is to help you realise your potential, awaken the fire within you, and forge ahead to take inspired action.

My desire, purpose, passion, and legacy is for you to awaken, activate, and align yourself to your innate magnificence and embrace the human experience.

I share with you a quote that I adore from Marianne Williamson, one that I feel will resonate deep within you and stir your soul.

> *"Our deepest fear is not that we are inadequate. Our deepest fear is that we are powerful beyond measure. It is our light, not our darkness, that most frightens us. We ask ourselves,*

*'Who am I to be brilliant, gorgeous, talented, fabulous?'
Actually, who are you not to be? You are a child of God.
Your playing small does not serve the world. There is nothing
enlightened about shrinking so that other people won't feel
insecure around you. We are all meant to shine, as children
do. We were born to make manifest the glory of God that is
within us. It's not just in some of us; it's in everyone. And as
we let our own light shine, we unconsciously give other people
permission to do the same. As we are liberated from our own
fear, our presence automatically liberates others."
~ Marianne Williamson*

Making Meaning Of Our Life

Sailing through life can easily lead us to focus on the inevitable drudgery and pain. We look around and the news is filled with cycles of war, terror, crime. It fills us with angst and fear, and it is all too easy to get caught up in these emotions.

Emotions are part of our human experience. Brené Brown speaks about emotions and experiences as layers of biology, biography, behaviour, and backstory. Many choose to be numb or avoid emotions; they attempt to push them down or away, fearing to feel, uncomfortable by their presence. Our emotions are not good or bad, they are a product of our human experience and act as a guide through life.

We cannot constantly chase happiness, but we also do not want to sink into the depths of despair as either would be an imbalance. Think of a pendulum: it doesn't swing one way constantly nor the other. It swings both ways, often evenly, and when it rests in the middle, it resets. So to with our emotions. Finding balance, creating harmony, and establishing equilibrium enables us to navigate our human experience with ease and flow.

This is how the Handbook for Being Human guides you. It helps you navigate through life: the ups, downs, emotions, experiences, conditioning, and un-become – all that you were 'taught' to be – to remember the powerful spiritual being that you are and live an abundant human experience.

I invite you to dive into this handbook, use the resources herein and apply your learnings into your everyday life. Engage daily, and you will feel compelled to move through to your next level of unfoldment.

It has often been said that this body of work is an antidote for life. However, I suggest we don't require an antidote for life. The definition of antidote is "a remedy to counteract the effects of a poison".

Life isn't a poison or something we need curing from. Quite the opposite.

Rather than finding a relief from life, an escape, or medicine to counteract life, I suggest we lean into life. Become a full and willing participant of your life. You are a powerful spiritual being; nothing can detract or 'remedy' this, nor would we want it to. By leaning in and connecting to your Higher-Self, living and knowing how powerful you truly are, you become co-creators with the Universe of your life. This is the work worth doing.

This playbook is about remembering your power, harnessing it, and becoming a conscious creator of your life: a co-creator with your Higher-Self and the Universe.

You now have a handbook for life, to guide you to accomplish this.

I am excited beyond measure for your journey. All you have to do is say YES, and embrace your journey and your life. I promise you wont regret it.

Sending you enormous amounts of love and energy,

Aida Jasmine

> "You are an infinite spiritual being having a temporary human experience."
>
> **WAYNE DYER**

1
Why Are You Here?

The Initiation

Congratulations on taking the next step to reclaiming your power and remembering the infinite potential that is within you.

You are about to embark on a soul-awakening, soul-activating, soul-embodying and soul- mastery journey that will exponentially amplify your human Earthly experience.

If you are ready to:

- Awaken to your Divinity and acknowledge more of who you truly are.
- Embrace your sovereignty, embody your true identity, and live authentically.
- Uncover your unique soul-gifts.
- Discover your soul-purpose and live a soul-led fulfilling life.
- Unlock and release limiting blocks and beliefs in your life,
- Take regular, grounded, soul-inspired action.
- Open yourself to the Universe and live a more joyful and abundant experience.

- Live a more empowered, purpose-filled life.
- And manifest from the soul.

Then keep reading. The initiation has begun.

Are you ready to connect with your inner light? Your soul is always calling you. It's time to awaken, connect deeply, embody your sovereignty, and allow yourself to shine and flow in tune with the Universe. Let me show you the way.

If you are ready to deepen the discovery of your soul, expand your life beyond your wildest dreams and live authentically, become more empowered, unstoppable, and unf@ckwithable, then this is for you.

This is a deep, sacred, soul journey within. You will be uncovering and dissolving your blocks, delays, and challenges and connecting with your Higher-Self, your soulful being, and living in alignment with your Spirit. You will learn to align with the Universe and manifest from the soul, your true source of abundance.

Throughout this sacred journey, your experience will include diving into:

- Uncovering your dharma, soul-purpose, spiritual gifts, and realising your infinite potential.
- Identifying your 'Why'.
- Discovering where your 'ego' may still be controlling your life – how it is actually holding you back from living your fullest potential, and how to release control with ease and grace.

- Learning some of the spiritual laws and principles of the Universe and how to apply them into everyday life for a more soulful experience.
- Aligning your gifts, path, and purpose with the Divine.
- Developing your unique soul-gifts and talents and how to share them with the world.
- Exploring why *SacredPlay* is an important part of your personal and spiritual development.
- Unearthing deep self-love and how it applies to our Spiritual journey.
- Harnessing and trusting your intuitive prowess and other super-powers.
- Understanding the transformative power of forgiveness and the role it plays in your spiritual development and path.
- Surrendering to the Divine and flowing with the Universe for a truly soulful, purpose-filled, and abundant life.
- Creating rituals to embody your learnings and curating a daily spiritual practice to develop self-mastery and become unshakeable.

We will be unlocking your unique soul's identity, your soul's unique highest blue-print, and your soul's purpose.

Time to strap yourself in and get ready for the ride of your life!

You will receive tools, tips, and tricks to reclaim your sovereignty, decode your soul whispers, and learn to lead by your soul to live a more joyful and fulfilling life.

As I mentioned before, this is your new playbook. Each chapter will contain *SacredPlay*, an opportunity for you to reflect on the lesson, gain wisdom, seek guidance from within, and integrate those lessons. This is how miracles appear in your life – when we harmonise our lessons, shift the paradox, and embody the new paradigm, magick happens.

This handbook is about discovering who you really are beneath it all: the stories we tell ourselves, the conditioning, the domestication, society's beliefs – everything that has led you to have beliefs about yourself. This journey is about un-becoming who you were told you SHOULD be and becoming who you truly are!

A quick note on the word 'should'. It is not a word I often use as it denotes a lack of choice. I will be reminding you regularly that you always have a choice. 'Should' is often how many of us were raised and taught – to believe our behaviour, words, and thoughts 'should' be a certain way. Many were told that we 'should' become something by our parents, such as a doctor, accountant, or some other suitable profession. We 'should' also behave a certain way or we 'should' do what is expected of us.

When I use the word 'should', it is rare and deliberate. I want you to believe you always have a choice. In fact, I will be encouraging you to question all your beliefs and all the 'shoulds' you were taught in order to uncover what is the truth of your heart and soul.

You maintain full sovereignty over your being and you choose your level of participation in the *SacredPlay*. You decide: enjoy the delicious power of choice. The outcome will resemble your decision and the level of your commitment to your growth.

This 'work' is not for the faint-hearted. A spiritual awakening can be shocking, painful, disruptive, challenging, but by far the most profound and rewarding 'work' you could do for yourself.

This work, to me, is delicious. Each lesson is a morsel to be savoured, relished, providing nourishment for my heart, mind, body, and soul.

Your mission, should you choose to accept it, is to awaken, activate, align, and discover your gifts. Your purpose in this lifetime is to use those gifts and be of service to humanity. My purpose is to help you to achieve this: to unwrap all that you 'know' about yourself, uncover your true infinite potential, and embody your sovereignty.

Everyone's development is unique. What may work for one person may be the exact opposite for another. You will receive various strategies, tools, tricks, and techniques to guide you towards your ascension and reclaim mastery over your being.

If you chose to be a full and willing participant, if you are ready to level up, live unapologetically, authentically, and with purpose and passion, then life will reward you beyond belief.

Are you still waiting for permission? If so, then allow me to grant you full permission to reclaim your Spirit, unleash your soul, and regain full self-mastery over your human experience – to live a life with infinite abundance.

Ignorance Is Not Bliss

Why do the work? Why wake up? It is much easier to slink back into your comfort zone, shut down, distract and numb yourself: just keep pointing the finger externally at experiences rather than go through the pain and discomfort that can lead to a spiritual awakening.

However, if you are truly committed to your spiritual journey, you know that this is not an option. The true pain and discomfort comes from not waking up, rather from staying numb. Life is meant to be fun, playful, loving, and abundant. If you are not experiencing this in all areas of your life, then there is work to be done.

It would be far easier to escape from the 'world' – retreat to the mountains, join a monastery, live in an ashram, and spend the remainder of days in prayer. However, not all of us are able to make such a commitment, nor may it be in your soul contract to do so.

If we are "infinite spiritual beings having a temporary human experience" as Wayne Dyer describes us, then it is up to us to make the most of this experience.

For example, when you take a holiday somewhere, do you go and just sit in the hotel room for the duration of your stay, then return home, not having seen or experienced your surroundings? You might say that would be a waste of a holiday. Whilst some might enjoy the rest, usually we like to make the most of our new destination by going out, seeing new sites, indulging in delectable delicacies, and engaging in different experiences.

This is the same with life. We can all to easily continue to repeat a cycle, staying stuck in the same pattern as if it were Groundhog Day. Often we choose this because it appears 'safe'. Or we could decide to delight in learning, growing, and expanding our human experience.

Much like a destination guidebook for your vacation, this handbook is a guide to help you navigate your human experience,. You will learn to develop daily practices and rituals into your everyday life to gain greater consciousness and awareness of your thoughts, patterns, and emotions while developing self-mastery. Awareness of self is our greatest gift. Once you have this, only then can you develop an awareness of others and all.

Spirit, God, Universe, Source, Cosmos, Infinite, Creator

A quick word on my terminology of Spirit, Universe, Source, Cosmos, the Infinite, God. Please use or read these terms interchangeably or add your own according to your belief system. This book is created to be non-denominational, to be used by all. For example, if you believe in a God, then please use that term where you read 'Spirit' or 'Universe', and vice-versa.

There are many names we use to call the Divine, always remembering that the Divine lives within. There is nothing external to you that does not first reside within you. If we are made in God's image, then we are also God-source energy. When a child is born, part of its DNA is sourced from its parents. I am suggesting so, too, are we: our Highest-Level Self is connected to All, Oneness. Our physical being is a small part of our Highest-Level Self, our Spiritual Being. We are Source, incarnated into a physical being, into this human body. You are not only created in God's image; you are part of God-self.

When We Know Better, We Do Better

Many travel through their daily lives without much conscious thought of what they are actually creating. It's likely we have been raised from a young age to believe that life is about death and taxes: we wake up, we go to work, we pay bills, and we die. We may have been led to think that life is meant to be a struggle. You may have even heard the expression, "Life is not meant to be easy."

Many of us had a predetermined career path laid out by our parents – what we 'should' do. Our thoughts, careers, and relationships are not always of our choosing. They are instilled within us from a very tender age by our parents, society, teachers, community; all well-meaning; however, often lethal.

Reflect for a moment what you did this morning. Wake up, bathroom, coffee, scroll through your phone, watch the news, go to work, lunch with friends/colleagues or at your desk, then home again to dinner, watch TV or Netflix, bed. Repeat.

Or perhaps you are one of the conscious few, who as soon as you wake up and before opening your eyes, you express heart-felt gratitude for your amazing life. Then, placing your feet on the floor, you express gratitude to Spirit and surrender to your soul purpose. Placing your hands on your heart in prayer position, you set an intention for the day: the beginning of your daily ritual.

To paraphrase the famous quote by Maya Angelou, "When we know better, we do better." When you reflect on those words you begin to understand that ignorance is not bliss. If we are choosing ignorance – and remember, doing nothing is a choice – then we are choosing to stay in the dark. We are choosing to not take responsibility for our actions or our life.

Many believe that life is simply happening to us and it's normal that we feel powerless. What an incredibly disempowering way to live. There is another saying, "knowledge is power," so, then, it is up to us to educate ourselves. But be selective in what you are educating yourself on too. If you are watching the news, then you are most likely being brainwashed by the media and constantly fed fear, scarcity, lack, and abandonment. If you are educating yourself by lifting the veil, then you are empowering your life and making more aligned and empowering decisions.

Knowledge in itself isn't power: applied knowledge is where true power lies. Educate yourself on how to live a more fulfilled, abundant life. The quality of your life is attributed by the quality of your questions – so practice asking better questions.

The popular book and movie The Secret opened a lot of people's minds to the law of attraction. Our thoughts become feelings; our feelings become actions; and our actions create our reality. Emotions are energy in motion. What does that mean? Let me break it down for you.

Your Thoughts Create Your Reality

You are a powerful creator. You are constantly manifesting. Look around you. Everything that is in your life or showing up in your life, you created: every experience, every person, everything. You can either feel empowered or disempowered by that revelation.

I encourage you to see this as empowerment. You have the power of choice. Knowing that you are a powerful creator and you are constantly creating is a very significant realisation. We will delve more into this later in the book.

How To Use This Handbook

It's important to think of practical ways to implement and integrate the secrets revealed in this handbook to quickly increase the quality of your life.

I encourage you to prepare space for yourself each day to reflect, activate, and align your learnings. Try to schedule time for yourself on a daily basis. I appreciate this may be challenging at first, however what gets scheduled, gets done. There is no right or wrong time to do this *SacredPlay*. Different times work for different people. Experiment and play with different schedules and see what works best for you. It's like throwing spaghetti at a wall to see if its cooked, try different approaches until one 'sticks' for you. If you are unaccustomed to taking time for yourself, then this at first may be challenging. Persist, until it becomes a habit.

Some of the greatest CEOs, leaders, influencers, and power-players on the planet maintain some form of schedule and always allocate a set amount of time for themselves each day.

Allow yourself to be a student and adopt a learner's mindset. Great Masters know that they are the perpetual student and are always open to learning. Read each chapter as if it is the first time you are receiving this information. It may be presented in a way that challenges a belief system, or you may resonate with it completely. You may receive many "AHA!" moments that bring revelations alongside several "ahh" moments, a soothing balm placed over a wound. Either way, be open to receiving new information.

Remember, it's likely you are going to encounter some hurdles come along your path, and these usually show up as:

- **Time:** not scheduling time aside for yourself each day as other 'priorities' seem to 'pop up'.
- **Motivation:** lacking motivation to 'do the work' and prioritising your needs.
- **Resistance:** mental blocks or a feeling of unworthiness preventing you from showing up.

Recognise these for what they are: blocks from your 'ego', resisting your soul's development and gaining self-mastery.

There are going to be times where you will feel triggered. Some of the teachings I am sharing with you may feel abrasive, strange, or even brutal. These lessons are designed to shake things up – for you to 'wake up'. If you are not feeling challenged, you are not breaking free of old patterns and behaviours.

"One cannot heal in the same place one got sick." You are here to break free from these chains, to release yourself from this prison, and to reclaim your freedom and sovereignty.

On the other hand, you may feel that this content fully resonates with you. I often feel spiritual tingles or goosebumps when I am reading or hearing something that resonates with my Higher-Self. I then align myself with these truths, integrate and embody them, and they then quickly become my new way of being.

There is a reason why you are here. It is time for you to reclaim your vision, integrate your learnings, and move forward, visioning and creating your life. It is time to awaken to your soul, activate your power, align with your Higher-Self, and embody self-mastery over your being.

Each chapter will have a series of *SacredPlay* homework activities for you to do. This is to integrate the learnings into your life and embody your expanded awareness and sovereignty.

I am not here to give you the answers. We are developing your innate wisdom, reminding you of your infinite potential, and connecting you back with it so that you may open up and receive the answers from within. Once again, all the answers are within you. I am here to help you reclaim your birthright as the sovereign infinite spiritual being that you are, guiding you to navigate this human experience.

I invite you to reflect on your intention for picking up this book and ask yourself two important questions:

- What do I want to receive from reading this book?
- What do I hope to achieve once I have completed this book?

Take some time for yourself to reflect on the questions and your intention. There is no right or wrong answer. We simply want to see what is underlying your intention.

Write your thoughts and findings down in the space below or grab a journal that will sit alongside this book. Record any of your thoughts, musings, findings, "aha" moments, and inspirations that you gain.

Remember, there is no judgement here. We simply want to witness what is being expressed at this time. Later, you will be able to reflect back to see how far you have come along this journey.

The time, energy, and effort you place into your lessons will be expressed by your growth and expansion. Only you have control over your experience and growth, and I encourage you to use this resource and energy wisely.

If you do not know how to respond to the questions or you are feeling stuck, that is OK. This playbook is about uncovering what wants to be unleashed in order to align with your Higher-Self and the Universe to live a truly fulfilled and abundant life.

Sacred Play

What do I want to receive from reading this book?

What do I hope to achieve once I have completed this book?

"Religion is for people afraid of going to hell.
Spirituality is for those who have already been there."

SIOUX

2
Remember Who You Are

What It Means To Be A Human Being

To understand what a hu-man being is, first we must look at the meaning behind the words. The root meaning behind HU is one of the ancient African names for God. The ancient Africans, also known as the 'sons of God', had a name for what MAN is. MAN, depicted in ancient hieroglyphs, translated into what resembles as 'humankind' or 'human-like'.

The ancient Greeks were also known as the sons of God and referred to a hu-man as a God-man.

This understanding of the word hu-man, then, refers to being God-like. Being God-like is a state of eternal love. The word BE-ing reminds us to simply BE, not DO. When we BE love, we don't have to DO anything: we are in a state of love and flow.

The term 'human being' reminds us of our God-self energy and God-like love. By simply be-ing our innate source energy, a 'human being', we are reminded that we are God-like (love) in its full and present state of BE.

Remember who you truly are: an infinite being of the Cosmos, God-source energy, a pure state of loving presence. I explore this further in a future chapter. The seed has been planted to remind you of your powerful Higher-Self.

Spirituality Versus Religion

This playbook is a guide for you to awaken to your spiritual prowess. It is not linked to any religious belief. It is important to understand the difference between religion and spirituality.

Religion, first of all, is a group experience: its main purpose is to protect the group, primarily from physical threats, disease, poverty, death, social crises, and even war. Religion is rooted in deep indoctrination and based on a fundamental set of beliefs. These beliefs are often based on a code of moral conduct for humans to follow.

Spirituality, on the other hand, is an individual experience directed toward releasing fears of the physical world and pursuing a relationship to the Divine.

My purpose here is not to argue for or against either side or viewpoint regarding religion or spirituality. I am here to guide you to what you feel resonates with your soul calling.

I believe you have a Divine purpose, a mission. You have chosen to come to this life; you have been granted a human experience, so you may as well enjoy it. The greatest opportunity given during our human experience is to uncover this Divine purpose and mission.

I believe everything is Divinely guided and you are now ready to reclaim your life.

You may be feeling the gentle pull of the Universe and are now ready to align with the desires of your soul and heart.

Spirit will continue to pull at you until the pain of not following your dharma, your soul mission, is more painful than the resistance. This was the case with me. The pain of not sharing this knowledge and wisdom contained in this book with others became more painful than staying quiet, small, and hidden. How could this be?

When you suppress your emotions, feelings, and purpose, it manifests as physical pain in your body. You begin to get sick; your body starts to develop dis-eases; you develop physical symptoms such as pain, headaches, migraines – and so it began with me. My body started displaying signs of physical pain: I was getting headaches and Spirit would continue to deliver these messages to me until I sat up and listened.

How many times have you had a moment in life and thought, what the…? Why did that happen? You are going about your day, minding your own business, and then life happens. Something triggers you, activates you, and throws you off course. You may be feeling stuck in some area of your life or you may even be at a stage in your spiritual journey where you are ready to transcend to the next level. You may wish to uncover your soul's purpose or learn the know-how on following it. You have come to this book for a reason. As you work through the handbook, these reasons may unfold.

A good guide does not tell you what to see; a good guide shows you were to look. I am here to guide you back home, to look inwards and reveal to you the innate power, wisdom, and strength that already resides within you, to realign you with your Higher-Self, Spirit, the Universe, God – and from that place, capture your purpose and live a Divinely guided life, one filled with joy, abundance, peace, and bliss: to live Heaven on Earth.

As you work through the handbook each day, you will begin to notice changes in your life. They may be subtle at first, but they count as changes nonetheless. You may experience a satori moment or it may be more kenshō – more on these elements later. I encourage you to journal daily. Don't worry, I have a whole chapter on journalling and how to create your life – yes, *create* your life – not just to survive, but thrive.

I want you to develop a practice that fits in with your beliefs, timetable, and what you believe you will be able to commit to and fulfil each day. There will be different levels of engagement as you move throughout the playbook. The first time you read this book, you may simply read it through without participating in any of the *SacredPlay* or follow any level of engagement. Then, as you are feeling pulled or called to, you may move to the next level of engagement and follow the activities in the *SacredPlay* until you are fully involved in all of the exercises and practices each day throughout your life.

You may wish to refer back to this book several times throughout your life: anytime you feel stuck or feeling pulled towards the next level of your unfoldment, maybe needing a little guidance and deeper self-reflection.

This isn't a book on manifesting or a 'quick-fix for life'. My intention in writing this book is to help you navigate this human experience, awakening you to your potential power and soul purpose. By doing this, you will naturally begin to create a more purposeful and fulfilled reality. You will begin to feel pulled towards a direction rather than pushed. You will begin to feel bliss and move about your day with a sense of peace rather than worry and fear.

Hierarchy Of Values

Myles Munroe is quoted to have said, "True leaders are born when you find something to die for." However, I would like to challenge this quote with this thought...

Find something to die for, then LIVE for it.

- Do you know what you stand for in life?
- Do you know what you will live for?
- Do you know what you will die for?

Your response to the above questions greatly impacts how you presently live your life. Consciously or unconsciously, your life will revolve around what you hold dear, what you live for, and what you die for.

You often hear people saying to "go with the flow". Many of us do, indeed, sail through life but often without conscious thought, succumbing to whatever others are doing or saying. Now, do not get me wrong, I LOVE flow, but only when it is in Divine alignment. There is a distinct difference between flow that is coming from the Universe when we are in alignment with our Higher-Self – that is positive flow. Then there is the flow where we simply go along with other people because we do not want to rock the boat. We feel like we have no choice; we don't want to stand out, or perhaps people pleasing seems the easiest way through life.

Our hierarchy of values stems from what we hold dear in life. What is tremendously important to us: our core values.

When you know who you are and what you stand for, the rest will unfold. My desire is for you to not simply be living or surviving your life. My sincerest and greatest desire for you is to be a full and willing participant in your life and to THRIVE. Stay attuned to your values, align with them, and design your life from your values.

On a side note, beware of falling into the martyr archetype. This archetype resembles someone who has a pattern of self-sacrifice and service to others, at their own expense. They often sacrifice their own needs and desires, in order to do things for others, from a sense of obligation or guilt. This behaviour can lead to feelings of anger, resentment and a sense of powerlessness.

There is no abundance or growth linked to martyrdom. This is a confined and restrictive space to live in. Instead, find your passion and purpose and live for it. Allow it to move you, excite you, inspire you, and in doing so, it will inspire the hearts and minds of others. Be so filled with passion and fire for your life that you wake each day excited and ready to embrace your abundant life.

In order to be inspiring, you must first BE inspired. This starts with knowing what you hold dear. Once you know your hierarchy of values, it will serve as inspiration daily. I invite you to refer to them daily, as you would your intention.

The purpose in establishing your hierarchy of values is to determine what is your higher purpose, what sets your soul on fire, and what enables you to live your infinite potential. Staying in alignment with these values and intentions will help reprogramme your brain, raise your vibration, and initiate a higher-habit for you to live an aligned, purposeful life.

Let us begin by establishing your hierarchy of values.

Firstly, ask yourself the following questions and reflect what comes up for you:

- What is really important to me?
- What are the things that make me feel like I am doing what I am placed on this Earth to do?
- What activities leave me feeling fulfilled and satisfied?
- What is it about these activities that make them so special?

Either in the space below or in your journal, write down your reflections. Make a list of all the things that are important in your life, what values you hold dear, and what is important to you. Trust the internal guidance and messages you are receiving. Write down what comes up without overthinking about it. Write down not what you think you 'should' do, rather what *really* wants to come through.

For example, here is a list of some core values that may help you with this *SacredPlay* task:

Safety	Money	Travel
Career	Health	Adventure
Family	Social	Collaboration
Routine	Friendship	Security
Beauty	Authority	Freedom
Self-Care	Recognition	Legacy

What values are important to me?

What do I hold most dear in my life?

Now that you have a list of your values, select your top 10 values from your list. This is not intended to be something that you would 'like' to have: it is at the core of your being, something you hold dearest.

Ask yourself, what is the most important thing in my life? What is uncompromising? Does family come before work and money? Continue to ask these questions and keep refining your list until you have a top 5. It is likely you will have more; however, our attention begins to dilute if we have more than 5 things we are focusing on. Your top 5 are usually hard to distinguish the rank between them, and that's great. We'll work through them more below.

Write your findings down.

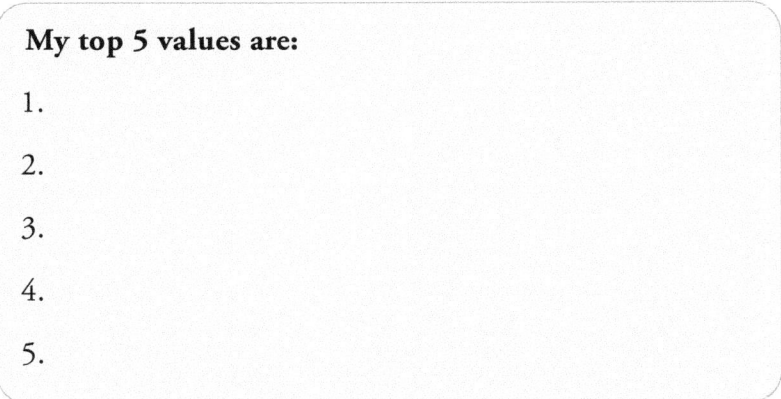

My top 5 values are:

1.

2.

3.

4.

5.

Get Zoned In

Great work. Now that you have zoned in on your hierarchy of values and have a top 5, the next step is to now write a story for each value or core system of belief. Write it as an affirmation or goal in the present tense. Write a positive affirmation or declaration for each value. This will help to embody this value into your life, where you become unwavering towards your path and purpose. Use the space provided below or grab your trusty journal and begin writing.

Example of a hierarchy of value statement.

Below is an example if you have 'family' as one of your hierarchy of values:

"I am so happy and grateful now that my family is all healthy and well. We are a strong family unit. We all share and show love and compassion for each other. We get along smoothly, have fun, and share with each other regularly."

You can go as in-depth as you wish. I like to get really clear on my values and go deep. However, if this is the first time you are going through this process, don't get overly bogged down in the detail. Remember, there is no right or wrong way to write this; simply stay positive and present with your words.

You may review these over the coming weeks and months, refining them as your vision becomes clearer. Rather than setting a New Year's resolution each year, feel free at any time to set an intention and review your hierarchy of values. When you revisit them, create a vision for each, taking time to visualise and meditate on them daily to integrate them into your life.

Read your hierarchy of values every day. Have them written somewhere visible so you are constantly reinforcing them into your subconscious. I personally have mine written on my mirrors of my wardrobe, so every time I am in my room, I am consciously and unconsciously taking in my core values.

Take time on a daily basis to visualise these values as if they are present in your life and meditate on them. The intention is to reprogramme your brain and instil higher-habits to enable you to live a life filled with passion and purpose. Epigenetics teaches us that our brain doesn't know the difference between what is real or what is a visualisation, so it is important to take time, daily, to visualise your values as if you are living them presently in the here and now. See them, feel them, live them.

> **Write an affirmation for your top 5 hierarchy of values. Remember to make them positive, affirming, and in the present tense.**
>
> **1.**

2.

3.

4.

5.

"No, we don't need more sleep. It's our souls that are tired, not our bodies. We need nature. We need magic. We need adventure. We need freedom. We need truth. We need stillness. We don't need more sleep; we need to wake up and live."

BROOKE HAMPTON

3
Soul Alignment

Living In Alignment With Your Soul

Our spiritual awakening is reconnecting us to our spiritual consciousness, helping us to remember who we are by living in alignment with our Soul or Higher-Self. Living connected with our Higher-Self enables us to flow through life, engaging fully in our human experience, and co-creating a life with the Universe on purpose.

There are four stages of spiritual awakening. I have listed these below to help you identify your soul alignment. To keep things simple, these stages can be classified as follows:

- TO me (victim consciousness)
- BY me (manifesting consciousness)
- THROUGH me (channel consciousness)
- AS me (BE-ing consciousness)

These stages are by no means linear and you may be in different stages in different areas of your life. Let's first dive in to understand each stage a little more and what these mean for you.

TO me (victim consciousness)

In this stage, we feel like we have no control of what happens in our life. We often feel that the things that happen to us are beyond our control. During this stage we may blame others for our life. For example, we may blame our parents for our upbringing, and as a result, we feel we don't have certain things in our life that we deserve. Or we blame an ex-partner, accident, divorce, boss, or someone else for where we are and what is happening to us.

Yes, I am sure you have a very convincing argument for each of these things. That is, in fact, the point of this stage. We are playing the blame game and pointing the finger outward. We feel we have no control of what is happening in our life, that life is happening *TO* me and I have no power. This stage is often our biggest trigger and the one we may need to work on the most. However, I promise you it is worth it.

BY me (manifesting consciousness)

This stage was made popular in recent times by the book and movie, The Secret. Since then, many law of attraction teachers have emerged, prescribing many ways for us to be conscious creators of our life. This is the stage we refer to as the 'manifesting consciousness' or the *BY* me stage. We are consciously manifesting or materialising our goals and dreams in the physical realm.

During this stage, we are 'focusing' our intentions on something we would like to create, for example, a new car, new job, more money, our ideal partner, and so on. Many think this is the sole purpose of our life; however, there is more. This is our 'human self' deciding on what we would like and setting our intention and focus on that one thing. This is a fun stage, and I encourage you to play with your intention and manifesting abilities.

THROUGH me (channel consciousness)

Through our quiet meditation, we often receive messages, insights, and visions. This guidance is from our Higher-Self, the Universe, or from a higher realm – whatever your belief is.

We refer to this as 'channelling consciousness' or the *THROUGH* me stage, where we are receiving these visions and messages from our Higher-Self and the Universe, enabling us to take inspired action towards those goals and dreams. We are consciously creating a life connected to Source energy.

AS me (being consciousness)

This is a beautiful stage where we are aligning with our Higher-Self and the Universe and living life by simply 'Being'. We are living fully present, in the moment – completely connected and guided by our Higher-Self and the Universe.

This stage is not to be confused with the TO me stage, where we feel we have no control over our life, pointing the finger outward, and playing the blame game. This stage is when we are in full alignment, retaining full sovereignty over our being, and living a blissful, connected, abundant, and prosperous life.

During this stage, all of our needs are met: mentally, emotionally, physically, spiritually, and financially. All of our desires and dreams are aligned with Source. We are living our soul's purpose, walking our path, and everything is available to us.

Remember, these stages are not linear. You may notice that in some areas of your life you are consciously manifesting or creating your life, while there are other areas where you still feel like life happens *to* you, without choice, like in the victim consciousness stage.

You may notice in other areas of your life, still, you may be consciously creating, channelling, or capturing a vision from your Higher-Self or Universe and taking inspired action on that vision.

Ultimately, we want to be focusing our energy and witnessing our life unfolding by simply 'being'. this is living in soul embodiment and personal mastery. We are one with our Higher-Self and the Universe, living aligned to our path and purpose.

Did you know that your subconscious mind doesn't know any other reality? Only yours. Whatever you feed your mind, the words you speak – either to yourself or others – is actually programming your mind. Think about that for a moment.

Even the words you think and say to other people, when you are sitting in judgement or gossiping about them, your subconscious mind actually believes you are speaking about, and to, yourself. Now do you understand the importance of feeding your mind, heart, and body only with high vibrational words, emotions, and actions?

Moving Beyond Shame, Blame, And Guilt

Shame is felt when we feel like we are 'bad'. When experiencing this feeling, the focus is on the self. We feel we must be inherently bad, that we are somehow flawed, unworthy of love, belonging, or connection. There is no transformative energy within shame, no driving force for change. This is because when we feel shame, the focus is on self.

When we feel guilt, the focus is on the behaviour that caused this emotion. We may feel we have behaved badly or failed to do something; maybe we feel we failed to act on our values. This emotion *can* incite change.

Blame is believing, "Life is happening to me," just like within the victim consciousness. You might say to yourself, "I have no control." This usually leads us to blaming others or pointing the finger outwards for our circumstances. When we are blaming others, we are giving away our power. When we take full responsibility for our actions, we can propel change. Change first begins within

Shame, blame, and guilt are egocentric emotions. They focus on the self and hold us in judgement and separation from others and our Higher-Self.

When we show love and compassion for our experiences, we transform these negative emotions into learning experiences. If you ever feel these emotions creeping in, ask yourself, "What can I learn from this experience?" or "What is seeking to emerge through me?" or "How can I grow?" or "If this situation weren't to change, how can I find my bliss?"

You are a Divine infinite being, having an Earthly human experience. You are unique, and you have gifts and talents waiting to emerge through you to share with the world. Transmuting shame, blame and guilt compels us to co-create with the Universe, take back our power and share our soul-mission on Earth.

How do you know what areas of your life are in alignment with your Higher-Self? We will work through each area of your life to establish where you are in alignment and what areas you are holding yourself back and feeling a 'victim'.

Sacred Play #1

Now that you have set your intention for this chapter, it is important to uncover where you are holding yourself back. We will look at each life structure within your life to uncover where you may still be playing the 'victim" or blame game, plus what areas you feel you have mastery.

Remember, there is no judgement. Be kind and compassionate to yourself during this process. We simply want to witness where you are at in life, which stage you are at in each pillar. Do this honestly and to the best of your ability. Only you will know the results, and we no longer need to lie to ourselves.

For this *SacredPlay* assignment, we will break it up into two parts. Part 1 will focus on each life structure, determining where we have mastery and where we may be sitting in victim mode. Once we have established our life structures, in Part 2, we will create higher-habits that support our vision and life purpose.

Let us begin.

Life Structure Review

This is an integral part of our soul embodiment and self-mastery journey. Only with honest self-reflection can we begin to transcend and embody our soul's purpose.

Find a quiet space and meditate for a few moments. Ask each of the following questions regarding each life structure and listen carefully to what emerges. It is important to simply witness this without judgement and to write down your findings.

Before we begin, evaluate your situation and do a self-assessment on where you rate yourself for each life structure on a scale of 1-10: 1 being in 'victim mode' or blaming others and 10 being in full alignment and mastery. You may then wish to refer back to this scale when you complete the book and see how your experience has shifted as your awareness has expanded.

Ask yourself the following questions for each life structure below:

- Where am I holding myself back?
- Where and what area of my life do I feel victimised or unworthy?
- Where do I feel mastery?

Do this for each life structure:

Spiritual
Ego
Beliefs
Relationships
Livelihood (work)
Body Temple
Money / Finances
Community

Life Structure Scale

Now using a pen or pencil, rate yourself on each structure by filling in the table below with a number between 1 and 10, where 1 is being in 'victim mode' or blaming others and 10 is being in full alignment with self-mastery. Remember, there is no judgement when doing these *SacredPlay* tasks. We simply want to uncover what is an underlying belief system.

Life Structure

Spiritual		
Ego		
Livelihood		
Body Temple		
Beliefs		
Relationships		
Money / Finances		
Community		

Now that you have given yourself a rating for each life structure, ask yourself the above questions and reflect on what emerges through you. Remember, the depth to which you choose to participate and dive into your subconscious and do the deep self-reflection will be evident from your results and compensated with the appropriate rewards. Some would consider this 'shadow work', diving into the unknown, into the subconscious, to unveil programming and changing what no longer serves and elevating to the new paradigm.

> **Life Structure - Spiritual:**
> - Am I holding myself back spiritually?
> - Do I feel victimised or unworthy in this life structure?
> - Do I follow others or conform to my upbringing that I have since discovered does not align with my true values?
> - Do I feel mastery in this life structure?

Life Structure: Ego

- Is my ego holding me back?
- Do I feel victimised or unworthy in this life structure? Do I allow my ego to control my life?
- Do I feel I have mastered my ego? Is my ego balanced?

Life Structure: Livelihood (how I make a living)

- Am I holding myself back in my livelihood, career, work?
- Do I feel victimised or unworthy in how I make a living?
- Do I feel I have following my purpose and mission with mastery in this life structure?

Life Structure: Body Temple

- How do I view my Body Temple? Do I love what I see when I look in the mirror?
- Do I feel victimised or hold unworthiness in my Body Temple? Do I seek external validation?
- Do I feel mastery in this life structure? *Do I love myself unconditionally and treat myself with compassion?*

Life Structure: Beliefs (what are my belief systems?)

- Are my beliefs holding me back? Are my beliefs my own, or from others, ie school, teachers, parents, religion, race, community, etc?
- Do I feel victimised or unworthy in my belief systems? Am I being overly rigid in my beliefs out of fear or failure?
- Do I questions my beliefs and feel mastery in this life structure?

Life Structure: Relationships

- Am I holding myself back in my relationships?
- Do I feel victimised or unworthy in my current relationships? Have I experienced feeling victimised or unworthy in my past relationships?
- Do I feel I experience conscious connections and mastery in this life structure?

Life Structure: Finances / Money

- How is my relationship with money? How do I feel about money?
- Do I feel victimised or unworthy regarding finances and money? Am I able to attract and save money with ease and flow?
- Do I feel I have a great relationship with money and mastery in this life structure?

Life Structure: Community

- Where and how do I see myself in my community?
- Do I feel victimised or unworthy in my community? Do I fully participate in my community and contribute?
- Do I feel I am of service to my community and mastery in this life structure?

Creating Higher-Habits

Having consciousness on where you are in your life structures is vitally important. By recognising and raising your awareness on the life structures that are supporting your life path and purpose, you can allow more space in your life for those that require expansion and focus.

Once you have answered the questions above and established where in your life structures you are experiencing mastery and where you may be playing victim, it is time to shift your habits that may be unconsciously *not* supporting your vision. We are going to start replacing your 'habits' with 'higher-habits'. Psychology tells us that a habit is a routine of behaviour that is repeated regularly, unconsciously. Part of our journey is creating higher-habits that serve you.

People focus on trying to break habits; however, this only perpetuates the habit as the focus is on what you are attempting to 'break'. Whatever you focus on, you receive more of. For example, if you are attempting to give up smoking, your focus is on smoking and not smoking anymore. All of your focus is on either smoking and not smoking. See how that just focuses on smoking? My mind went around in circles just writing that, hence the repeated pattern that doesn't serve. The focus here, then, is on smoking, not the solution.

A more positive and aligned behaviour is switching your habits that no longer serve you with a higher-habit that is more in alignment.

This is important in articulating your vision. By creating and instilling higher-habits, your vision begins to emerge, and you can let go of limiting beliefs. We do this through daily practice.

Through this daily practice, we begin to take back our mind. Our thoughts create our reality, which is why the alignment of our thoughts is so important. If the focus is on changing a habit, we can do this through the methods listed below. I encourage you to utilise these methods and see which one works best for you. Different methods will work better with different habits; see which one suits. You may use several methods combined.

Gratitude

Express gratitude daily. It is the fastest way to transmute your mood, boost energy, and raise your vibration. It is easy to focus on the negative; however, there is much in our lives to be grateful for. Begin your day with listing 5 things you are grateful for. Practice gratitude throughout the day. Gratitude shifts our vibration immediately and helps place our focus on positive things in our life.

Meditation

Spend at least 15 minutes each day in quiet meditation. Focus on your breath, then on your body. Allow your mind to quieten. by doing this, we allow messages and guidance to come through. It also allows visions to flow through from our Higher-Self and Source Energy.

Visualisation

This practice enables us to visualise all the good things we would like to create in our life. This is particularly useful and fun in the 'manifesting' or BY me stage of our consciousness. Spend a few minutes each day on how you would like your day to flow. Visualise yourself living the life of your dreams: immerse yourself and really feel, taste, touch, and smell the vision.

Have the right conversations (with ourselves and others)

Your words have power and create your reality. The word abracadabra literally means, "I will create as I speak." Be mindful of your words as they reinforce and create your life.

Affirmations

Mantras and affirmations are positive statements that imprint and reprogramme your subconscious mind. They are designed to trigger emotional responses that promote healing and raise your vibration.

Declarations

A declaration to the Universe states your intention and/or what you are ready to call into your life. For example, "I am open, ready, and available for more good in my life than I have ever imagined."

You, beautiful soul, are worthy of living a fulfilled, aligned life. One that is from your soul. It is your birthright.

Mahatma Gandhi once said, "Be the change you wish to see if the world." Change begins with you.

Sacred Play #2

Reflect on your responses to each life structure and review where in your life you have established habits that may not be serving you and where you can shift these to higher-habits. A habit is something that we do repeatedly, without conscious thought. They can either serve us or not. By shifting these unconscious thoughts and patterns to conscious ones, we can then 'change' our habits that do not support our journey to ones that serve us.

This takes consistency, but using the tools listed above, it will help to heal, transmute, and transcend our habits to serve us better.

Use the table below as a checklist of higher-habits that you can begin integrating each day that serve you. Go through each life structure on the following pages, asking yourself each question to bring greater awareness and creation of a higher-habit.

Don't be limited by the example question, though. Ask yourself more questions. Ask yourself empowering, open questions. The quality of your questions directly impacts the quality of your life. Examples are provided in each life structure below in the *SacredPlay* for you to follow.

Integrating Higher-Habits

Life Structures

Spiritual

(How can I connect spiritually, with my Higher-Self and the Universe each day?)

Ego

(How can I balance my ego?)

Livelihood

(How can I draw more abundance into my life?)

Body Temple

(What if my body could heal anything?)

Beliefs

(What truth is there in my beliefs? Are my beliefs my own?)

Relationships

(How can I consciously attract more like-minded connections in my life?)

Money & Finances

(How can I draw more financial prosperity into my life?)

Community

(How can I be more of service to my community?)

In order to integrate your learnings, it is important to establish daily rituals that will enable you to embody your new higher-habits. Reprogramming your subconscious to serve you and align with your new paradigm is how we make the shift, one that is long-lasting and worthy of you.

"The key to growth is the introduction of higher dimensions of consciousness into our awareness."

LAO TZU

4
Navigating The Different Dimensions

Navigating 3D And Beyond

When you know that you are a spiritual being having a human experience, you understand that there is no duality, no separation, and no good or bad.

This may be challenging in our 3D world as we are living what is. This 3D realm keeps us separated from one another, isolated, having feelings of unworthiness and feeling stuck. Duality keeps us stuck, and we add meaning to our suffering. It opens doorways to pain, illness, dis-ease and sorrow, allowing yourself to believe this is acceptable.

In this paradigm, it is difficult to understand other dimensions. Outlined below is each dimension from the first dimension to twelfth dimension. I ask you to open your mind and see the possibilities of what these can hold for you.

Your infinite spiritual being and Higher-Self knows these to be true. It is connected to all oneness. As your understanding and knowledge grows, your human experience will flourish and miracles will begin appearing in your life.

The brief description of each dimension below is there to demonstrate that there is more than our physical, Earthly existence. Remembering and connecting with other dimensions reminds us of our infinite power, potentiality, and that we are an interconnected spiritual being.

First, we require an understanding that a dimension is a state of consciousness and each dimension houses laws and principles specific to the frequency of that dimension.

The 12 Dimensions

- **1st Dimension:** The seed of creation. Our physical reality, such as planets, Earth, air, water, and all physical elements. This is the realm of quantum physics.
- **2nd Dimension:** The seed of information that represents life, our biological connection, such as the plant and animal kingdoms.
- **3rd Dimension:** This is the realm of our physical form, where matter and our physical reality exists. We attempt to prove that reality exists with our logical mind and give reason and explanation to thoughts and things.
- **4th Dimension:** This is the realm of time and of our emotions, our psychic and astral plane. This is the dimension of the subconscious mind and we also dream here.
- **5th Dimension:** This is the realm of Spirit and our unconscious mind. This is Light body awareness and remembering you are a multidimensional being. Only love resides here, and we remember our Higher-Self and oneness here. You recognise you are the creator of your reality.

- **6th Dimension:** This is the realm of the soul. Peace and balance and communication reside here. All language and symbols are housed here, along with astrological and genetic codes, and DNA templates. It also houses the Akashic records: the complete files on everyone and everything.
- **7th Dimension:** This is the realm of Infinity, where pure Light and vortexes reside. Pure creativity and expression expand as the soul tunes in to evolve itself.
- **8th Dimension:** This is the realm of eternity, group souls, and oceans of Light consciousness. All focus, information, form, time, spirit, soul, infinity, and eternity are united. It is the Universe itself. This is where astrology, numerology, and crystal codes information resides while sacred geometry is utilised.
- **9th Dimension:** This dimension represents planetary formations, where galaxies, planets, star systems, dimensions, and more take form. It contains the underlying currents of astrology and numerology, understanding the causes and dynamics beyond 8D.
- **10th Dimension:** This is the dimension of the Multiverse, where greater cycles and continuous expansion and growth of consciousness resides, encompassing the Truth and the Universe. This is the upper creation realm where our spirit comes into creation. It is the Home of Elohim.
- **11th Dimension:** This is the state before creation, the realm of the Omniverse. The potential and state for all creation of spirits, forms, and Universes.

- **12th Dimension:** This dimension and vibration of love that penetrates through everything and unites All. Oneness with Source. The one point where all consciousness is One.

All human beings are multidimensional beings of Light. We have a dense physical body – which you know to be your Body Temple – and it houses some of our consciousness.

It is important to note that the 'higher realms' do not replace the 'lower realms'. Each layer builds on top of the previous one, creating a solid foundation, much like a pyramid. Developing a strong foundation in each level will enable you to ascend to higher dimensions.

Sacred Play

This chapter highlights that there is more than one realm and there is more than our physical human experience.

Reflect on what it feels like to learn about other dimensions and write your feelings below.

What does it feel like to be open to other dimensions?

What could this mean to your physical human experience?

"Mastery over others is strength,
mastery over yourself is
true power."

LAO TZU

5
Developing Self-Mastery

What Is Self-Mastery?

Self-mastery is self-control, self-discipline, self-awareness, and self-responsibility over one's impulses and desires. Self-mastery is monocle focus on areas of your life that you have control within, namely your thoughts, responses, and behaviours. You no longer have to place focused consciousness or awareness on an area of your life, as that area of your life is conditioned, whether this be physical, emotional, mental, or spiritual. Self-mastery is to know thyself. As you develop self-mastery over each area of your life, this transforms into soul-mastery.

This is living in alignment, living authentically.

What does it mean to be authentic? The Cambridge English Dictionary defines it as, "the quality of being real or true".

We are being authentic when our actions align with our core values and beliefs. Being authentic is being in sync with our Higher-Self. In order for you to live a fulfilled, purposeful life, it is important to live authentically. This simply cannot happen if you are wearing a 'mask' or pretending to be something you are not. We will uncover the belief systems that are not in alignment.

Earlier, we uncovered that a belief is a thought or premise that we feel strongly attached to and place our faith and trust in, whether it is serving us or not. Some beliefs we may have adopted from others: our parents, teachers, peers, friends, etc.

A belief does not have to be 'real' for us to have an attachment to it. For example, many hold the belief that the Earth is flat, whilst others hold the belief that the Earth is round, and both hold strong convictions in their beliefs. Now, I am not here to argue either way. Whatever your belief system is, we are here to uncover some of your beliefs and determine whether they serve for or against your life purpose.

We make decisions and choices every day, some consciously, though, many unconsciously, either through programming, default, instinct, or conformity. Many of our daily choices are made through our subconscious mind, with approximately less than 10% made consciously.

Conformity is our 'creative death'. Conscious choice is a function of our expanded awareness. Authenticity is a function of choice.

When we make conscious choices, we are living more authentically and in alignment with our soul. Living authentically is essential to embodying our Higher-Self and developing self-mastery.

Authenticity equals freedom. When we let go of masks, possess self-mastery, and reclaim full sovereignty over our being, we feel free – ready to fully express ourselves and what is wanting to emerge through us.

Freedom is our birthright. We are already 'free'. This is not something to attain; it is a belief system of our reality. Even if one is incarcerated, whilst you may be physically detained and confined, your mind and soul are still free to live authentically while expressing self-mastery. How we respond in situations is an act of consciousness and self-mastery.

Self-mastery can be obtained by focusing on the four keys below in your life. They encompass all aspects of your life structures and will navigate you towards living authentically with self-mastery. By gaining self-mastery over these four keys in your life, you will experience true freedom and live in alignment with your soul.

Key #1. Self-Reflection

Key #2. Self-Discipline

Key #3. Self-Responsibility

Key #4. Self-Awareness

Gaining self-mastery will actualise your full potential. Let's review these keys further and uncover how they are expressed in your life.

Key #1: Self-Reflection

It is important to reflect on your beliefs mentally, emotionally, physically, and spiritually in each life structure. This is not an exercise to beat yourself up on in areas that you may be letting yourself down, but this is necessary work to gain insight into what areas you are achieving mastery and where, presently, requires more focus.

For example, where are you currently sitting with your money and finances? How do you feel about money? What are your beliefs around money? Another important factor to consider is what value do you place on your desire, your money, finances, and abundance?

Here are some questions for you to reflect on with regards to your money and finances:

- What do you say about money when you talk to yourself, your inner dialogue?
- What do your parents, friends, and family say about money?
- What did you hear about money as a child growing up?
- How do you feel when you spend money?
- What emotion comes up when you think about money?

Your formative years from 0-7 years of age imprint your belief systems and will remain a factor in controlling your life until you recognise the patterns and make a conscious effort to shift them. For example, to uncover some deep-seated money blocks, think back to when you were 7 years old, what were some of your beliefs around money? This has formed a money blueprint in your subconscious for your life, until you consciously change it.

Listed below are some common belief systems surrounding money that many of my students have reported on, and some of which I personally previously believed in, until I shifted my mindset:

Developing Self-Mastery

- Money doesn't grow on trees.
- Money is the root of all evil.
- Money is hard to come by.
- I can't afford that!
- People with money are all bad.
- You have to work hard to get money.
- Rich people are greedy.
- People always argue about money, or the lack of it.
- I just want to help people; I don't care about money.
- I don't deserve money.
- Rich people or people with money are corrupt.
- People won't like me if I have a lot of money.
- I attract people who only want me for my money.

Do any of these statements resonate with you? Would you like to challenge any of these statements? Would you like to shift and change these beliefs if they hold true for you? I invite you to write in your journal what you think and feel regarding money. Freely express yourself in your journal, this is how we uncover our subconscious money blueprint.

You can ask similar questions regarding each life structure to uncover your core beliefs. Change the words 'money and finances' to 'relationships' or how you feel about your body and you will uncover fundamental beliefs.

If you find yourself not living your dreams, then something is out of alignment: heart, mind, body, or soul. Self-reflection gives us an opportunity to uncover underlying beliefs, unpack them, and shift them permanently.

I believe in aligning all four keys of your reality. It is not just one that you need to master, all four keys need to be put into alignment. When the belief of your mind matches the truth of your heart, everything will fall into place.

People are often afraid of their own potential. What if you were to have all of your desires materialise into physical reality? What would that look like? What would that feel like?

That reality actually scares many people, which is what is deep in your subconscious.

Self-reflection helps uncover the truth of your heart; that is where your soul resides and holds your highest potential. Once you have uncovered what is holding you back from what you desire, you can clear the outdated belief system, release limiting beliefs for good, and replace it with a higher-habit.

Your beliefs are your mind's most powerful manifestation tools. Align to the belief of your heart and soul and create a reality you love. Live a life of full abundance, aligned to your highest potential.

Key #2: Self-Discipline

Self-discipline is another key to experiencing self-mastery.

When we lead a life with self-discipline, we know our worth; we prioritise what is important to us, and we make choices that are aligned with our Higher-Self, purpose, and hierarchy of values.

By making choices through expanded awareness, we are doing what we say and saying what we do. These choices are made through self-discipline.

When practising self-discipline, it is important to develop a level of love around what you are doing.

Love what you 'have' to do and love what you 'get' to do.

The difference between 'have' and 'get' is through choice. Make your choices through expanded awareness and you'll find that you 'love what you do' because you 'get' to do it.

I hear you saying, "There are some things in my life that I 'have' to do; I don't have a choice: I 'have' to pay rent, phone bills, electricity, go to work, etc." I challenge you for a moment and reflect: do you really 'have' to do those things? Or do you 'get' to do all these things and experience the many benefits of them?

When we are sitting in the space of 'have to' rather than 'get to', we are staying in the 'victim consciousness' or blame mode. We already know this is not a transformative space. We want to expand and grow. It is necessary to shift away from 'victim consciousness' to one that is more expansive and empowering. What do you 'get' to do today? By just shifting to this expanded awareness, we begin to create and visualise what we do want to do and what we 'get' to do so we live a fulfilled, blissful, and abundant life.

Consider what areas in your life structures where you are feeling that you 'have to' do things. Then reflect on what you 'get to' do. Can you imagine shifting these mindsets and embracing that we 'get' to do a lot more than we think? We have a *SacredPlay* activity to do later regarding this, that will enable you to dive a little deeper to uncover and shift any victimhood and blame that is within you.

Key #3: Self-Responsibility

Responsibility means 'being able to respond'.

Being self-responsible means taking responsibility for your choices and actions and how you are responding to those. Sounds simple, right? However, this is not about shifting blame or responsibility to others, nor is it finding others to blame for situations in our life.

Real responsibility is responding to situations with love, peace, bliss, joy, laughter, or forgiveness, all coming from our Higher-Self and the Universe: the infinite oneness.

Our Key #1, self-reflection, gives us an opportunity to determine how we respond in each life structure. When we are self-responsible, it develops self-mastery and brings us freedom. We make choices based on our expanded awareness and we take responsibility for those choices. This brings us a sense of peace and freedom to our lives.

Are you truly being self-responsible for your choices, decisions, actions, behaviours? Where in your life can you be more self-responsible?

Key #4: Self-Awareness

Many believe that self-awareness is the image we project to the world. They place a large emphasis on how they look, their dress, on their appearance, or the 'image' they present to the public eye. This projection of an image is overly concerned with how one looks on the outside, rather than focusing more on what is going on inside.

We see this a lot on social media. Countless images of grand lifestyles, seemingly perfect appearances, opulent accessories, etc. Whilst for many this definition of self-awareness may be true, I challenge you to shift your paradigm and think about what *true* self-awareness is.

Now, there is nothing wrong with maintaining your physical appearance. In fact, it is an act of self-care and self-love, and I fully encourage this. When it is done in the right way, it is important; however, true self-awareness lies much deeper than our physical appearance.

Reflect on what image you are projecting into the world. What are your reasons for this image? Are you seeking 'likes' and 'followers' on social media? Are you doing it for attention and affection? Are you seeking external validation to make yourself feel better? Do you rely on this image and overly care about how others may see you?

True self-awareness is about being conscious of your thoughts and of your words without self-judgement. Being self-aware is allowing yourself to be more 'aware' of your true self, of what is real and authentic in you, and making choices based on this expanded awareness – then taking self-responsibility for those choices, not the image you present to the world or the 'roles' you may play.

Aligning with these four keys within yourself is integral to claiming self-mastery, living authentically, reclaiming your sovereignty, and realising your infinite potential.

Boundaries

Our Earthly experience is all about connecting. Boundaries are an essential part of allowing our experience, connecting with others to flow with compassion and empathy. Boundaries form the basis of our experience and provide clear guidance on where we end and another begins.

"Daring to set boundaries is about having the courage to love ourselves, even when we risk disappointing others." - Brené Brown

Setting boundaries holds ourselves and other people accountable for their behaviour. By holding our behaviour accountable, we are displaying self-mastery. When we don't set clear boundaries, we often feel others may be taking advantage of us, walking all over us, or hurting our feelings.

When a boundary is set, we can feel hurt or denied, believing that our feelings or emotions cannot be truly expressed or accepted. However, it is often the behaviour or expression of the feeling or thinking that is crossing the boundary.

Boundaries provide clear parameters for behaviour, and they invite in compassion and non-judgement.

For example, it's OK to have someone disagree with you; however, it is not OK to ridicule someone's ideas or beliefs.

Reflect for a moment on the things that you feel you 'have' to do. Write them down below or in your trusty journal.

Ask yourself the following question:

> **Where in my life do I feel I do not have a choice and I 'have to' do things?**

Reviewing your response to the above question, now ask yourself this one:

If this situation were to not change, how can I find bliss?

Meditate for a few moments, reflect on the above question, and write down what comes to you, without judgement. Simply witness and write it down.

We develop self-mastery by managing our responses to situations and by aligning with our Higher-Self. When we self-reflect, are self-aware, self-disciplined and self-responsible, we begin to shift our outdated belief systems to ones that are aligned with our hierarchy of values. When we are living in alignment, we experience freedom, which brings us a sense of bliss.

Now that you have reflected on developing self-mastery, I invite you to write down some strategies on how you can embody these four keys into your life structures, mentally, emotionally, physically, and spiritually, with your expanded awareness and knowledge.

For example, ask yourself what simple strategies can you put in place each day to make choices on expanded self-awareness? Write down your strategies in the spaces provided below or grab you beloved journal and let yourself flow, pen to paper, antennae to the Divine.

What daily strategies can I put into place to enable deeper self-reflection?

What strategies can I put into place to embody self-discipline?

What daily strategies can I put into place to develop self-responsibility?

What daily strategies can I put into place to develop greater self-awareness?

"There are only two emotions, fear or love. Go with Love."

WAYNE DYER

6
The Four Interior Pillars

The Four Interior Pillars

We have learned about the four keys to developing self-mastery: self-reflection, self-discipline, self-responsibility, and self-awareness. Now, I would like to introduce you to the four interior pillars.

We have all heard the expression, "Follow your heart but take your brain with you." I would like to suggest that this is only half of your 'being', only half of what makes you whole. Many follow their heart, others their head; however, in order to live a truly abundant, fulfilled, purposeful life, I would like to introduce you to the four interior pillars that I believe make us whole.

- Mind
- Heart
- Body Temple (Health)
- Spirit (Soul)

You may wish to associate them to the four elements: Air, Water, Earth, and Fire. The fifth element, Ether, can be considered to be your Higher-Self and the Universe. We need all the elements to create coherence, balance, and the ability to enjoy our Earthly existence.

Our mind, heart, body, and spirit or soul all make up who we are. These need to be in alignment in order for you to follow your path and walk this Earth with passion and purpose. This will enable you to develop greater self-mastery and embrace the human experience fully.

These interior pillars form a structure for your entire life. Think of these as your foundation. Anything with four legs or pillars creates a solid foundation. This is the same with your interior pillars.

Let us go through them below:

Mind

Many believe it all begins and ends with the mind. The job of the mind is to secrete thoughts. Many do not feel like they can control their mind. This is where positive affirmations, mantras, and a positive mindset will change your reality and create a more abundant, positive, fulfilled life.

Meditation can also help with this. A common myth is that meditation is practiced in order to 'stop' your thoughts, but this would be impossible. That's like imagining that you could hold back the waves of the ocean; it simply can't be done. Meditation, instead, is intended to help quieten the mind, resist the monkey-mind, lengthen the gap between thoughts, and give you more peace.

Your attitude to life and its challenges has a direct impact on what you create and manifest into your reality. Perspective is everything. By developing an attitude of gratitude, you will find that when facing challenges, you will be able to quickly shift energy into a higher vibration than your present thought. Whenever you find yourself having a 'negative' thought, quickly change the thought into a positive one, and keep following that energy.

Having a positive mindset is fundamentally important. Your mind will also affect your epigenetics, which is your behaviours and patterns. Epigenetics can change the way your body reads your DNA. By maintaining a positive mindset and being grateful, you can affect and transform your behaviours and patterns. A way to influence this is by keeping a gratitude journal. This can keep your mindset positive and working favourably for you.

Heart

If we are focused overly on our mindset and ignore our heart space, we are only really focusing on a small part of our whole being.

Reflect for a few moments on your emotional life. Are you stuck in the past? Do you regularly ruminate or feel anger, insecurity, trauma, or resentment about past events? Maybe you feel inadequate, blaming others for your misfortunes in life? This all leads to self-sabotage and imbalances in life.

Often, we are attempting to fill an emotional void with things like money, material things, sex, shopping, or external validation. These are only a temporary measure and do not ever really successfully fill a void in our life. After indulging in one of these actions, we may feel good again for a few minutes or hours, but then we need more. We become like an addict who is constantly looking for their next fix; we are constantly trying to fill the void in our heart with outer distractions.

We can work on and heal our heart space through emotional transformational techniques such as journalling, meditation, spending time in nature, massage, body work, and energy work, as well as through forgiveness.

Healing your heart will help you to live in harmony with others. Forgiveness plays a big part in this. By letting go of the past, healing our heart, releasing trauma and emotional holes, we begin living in alignment with our Higher-Self. We can be truly happy for others and live an abundant, fulfilled, purposeful life.

Body Temple (Health)

You can have a positive mind and have healed your heart space; however, your health and body are also vital and contribute another key pillar in creating a healthy and strong foundation.

Dis-ease, pain, and discomfort are all trapped emotions and energy in the body. Emotions are energy in motion; hence e-motion. Emotions are designed to flow, when we feel stuck or ill, this is usually as a result of trapped emotions. These can greatly impact the quality of your life and your ability to fulfil your purpose. Therefore, it is important to also work on your physical being and health.

Your energy is your greatest asset in creating, delivering, and living your purpose. You need fire to execute what you want to get done. A fire in your belly, your sacral chakra, is the source of you materialising your creation in the physical realm.

We all want to attain health, wealth, and happiness. Working on your energy, fitness, and vitality will lead you there. Hippocrates once said, "Let food be thy medicine and medicine be thy food." So it also stands to reason, "You are what you eat." Begin treating your body like a temple and be mindful of what fuel you are placing in your body. Would you put garbage in a temple or sacred space? Would you fill it with rubbish, not care what it looks like, and not maintain it? The same can be said with your physical body, your Body Temple.

By being mindful of what you put in your body and how you take care of it is not only an act of self-love, it will affect your heart, mind, and health as well.

It is important to take your health seriously. We only truly value our health when we are sick. Do something every day for your health. Treat your body like a temple, fuel it with high vibrational and nourishing food. Care for your physical body. Do some movement along with your affirmations, mantras, and meditate daily. This will help align your mind, heart, and body, activating health and vitality.

Spirit / Soul

Our Soul, Spirit, or Higher-Self is our fourth pillar in aligning our entire being and creating a solid structure or foundation for life. Aligning our head, heart, health, and soul is critical in creating a life on purpose. We do this by spending time in quiet meditation, connecting with our Higher-Self and the Universe, and getting clarity on our purpose.

When we are connected, we realise we are all one. By connecting with our Higher-Self, the Universe, Mother Earth, and all, we realise everything and everyone is a part of us. By hurting others, we are only hurting ourselves. By being soulful and connected with all, we understand we are here to be of service to others and serve humanity.

Our purpose calls us to live in alignment, and we can only truly do this when we are connected with our Higher-Self, the Universe, Mother Earth, and all.

Sacred Play

Spend a few minutes in quiet meditation and reflect on your four interior pillars. How are your Mind, Heart, Body Temple (Health) and Spirit / Soul? Reflect on all that you have learned so far and consider how you can align your four pillars on a daily basis.

You have learned how meditation and affirmations can shift energy, develop self-mastery, and change epigenetics. Contemplate what daily changes you can begin to make to align these four pillars.

Ask yourself these questions and remember to only witness, without judgement, what you discover about yourself. Journal your responses or write them in the space provide below.

Where am I out of alignment in my four pillars: head, heart, body (health), and soul? Am I always in my head? Am I currently suffering from any dis-ease or pain in my body? Am I holding on to past hurts, anger, and resentment?

What habits that no longer serve me can I change? What higher-habits can I create that serve me?

For example: What habits serve me well? Could they serve me better in some way?

What rituals can I put into place to stay in alignment?

(For example: meditate daily, keep a gratitude journal, conduct daily visualisations)

What self-love practices can I embrace to ensure I am working on my head, heart, health, and soul?

(For example: setting healthy boundaries, not participating in gossip, practising forgiveness, nourishing my Body Temple)

What practices can I put into place when I resort back to self-sabotage or attempt to fill the void with external influences?

(For example: show self-compassion and kindness, forgive myself, uncover the hurt or pain and heal this part of myself)

Love Versus Fear

Our subconscious mind is designed to move towards pleasure and avoid pain. Our mind is literally programmed to stop us doing anything that it has never done before. It is designed to avoid anything new because it cannot navigate the risk and hence, would rather keep us playing small.

I believe that all thoughts, emotions, and actions stem from either one of these: love or fear. When we are living from a space of love, it feels grounded, abundant, flowing, compassionate, and it resembles our Spirit.

When we are living from a space of fear, it feels anxious, comparative, jealous, scarce, guilty, and disconnected from our Spirit. This is where our ego plays and thrives.

Living in fear is a false paradigm. Fear triggers a stress response in our physical body. It is sometimes said the definition of FEAR is: False Evidence Appearing Real.

Our body is designed to live in love, not fear. We come from love; we are love. That is what Be-ing is and means, pure love. Just BE. When we return to this state, our lives transform and we create a new world and life. This is when magick and miracles happen.

When we come from fear, it is often ego based. When we come from love, we trust that everything will work out for us.

We can thank our ego for doing a great job in keeping us safe, albeit sometimes, a little too safe because it can keep us stuck and in repeating cycles.

Just a quick word on 'ego'. It is not a dirty word or a 'bad' part of us; it is not our shadow side or separate identity or being. The ego is here to show us the duality of consciousness, love or fear. When our ego is imbalanced, it keeps us separate. It will limit you and continue with thoughts and actions that we know to be self-sabotage.

Your ego is made up of all the beliefs, domestication, attitudes, and assumptions you have held about yourself and 'believe' to be true. This is an illusion. Remember the definition for FEAR: False Evidence Appearing Real? You are an infinite spiritual being, created in Love. Anything other than this knowing is an illusion.

We want to create harmony and balance with our ego so that you can shine your brilliance out into the world and live your purpose.

This is where visualisation, affirmations, mantras, and creating higher-habits can help shift us from fear to a space of love. When we program our subconscious mind with love affirming statements, thoughts, visions, and patterns, it will shift our programming to one of love, creating inspired actions and higher-habits, delivering miracles into our life daily.

Create some love affirming affirmations, mantras, and declarations to help keep you in a Love state. Use these for when you feel fear and recite them daily.

Here are some that may be useful:

- I am Love.
- I am Loving.
- I am Loved.
- I am Loveable.

"Choose your intention carefully and then practice holding your consciousness to it, so it becomes the guiding light in your life."

ROGER DELANO HINKINS

7
Living With Intention

What Is An Intention?

We often hear the word intention being referred to, telling us to live an 'intentional life' or to 'live with intention'. But what does that actually mean?

Gaining a greater understanding of what intention means, and how living with an intention, as Hinkins states, "so it becomes the guiding light in your life", will enable us to apply it to our lives.

Our 'intention' is the ability to focus on a core belief or value, and then to align our actions towards that intention accordingly.

Anyone can live with intention; however, it does require our focus and energy. If we are not living with intention, then we are allowing others to guide us through our life, often resulting in unwanted outcomes. Living with intention creates a purpose-filled life.

What Does Living Intentionally Look Like?

Living with intention enables us to build our life around our hierarchy of values and core beliefs. It is not living whimsically, merely existing, or just surviving. Living intentionally enables us to be guided by our values, take inspired action, and live a purpose-filled life.

Setting intentions allows you to choose your life, dictate your actions, and co-create with the Universe. An intention comes from deep within us. It is not spurred on by external values, what others are doing or thinking, or external resources. It directs you to be sincere, guides you to what lights you up, what your core values in life are, and how you imagine your life to be.

Use your hierarchy of values to set an intention each day, or the tone of your life, and let that be your 'guiding light'. You can use your hierarchy of values as a base for your life, and choose to set a daily intention, to align and shift focus on a particular area of your life where you are desiring growth and expansion.

Living with intention takes energy and effort. It requires us to be persistently conscious of our thoughts and actions. It requires us to be grounded, focused and fully present in the now. This is living an intentional, purpose-filled life.

6 Steps To Living Intentionally

I have listed 6 easy steps below to help you begin living an intentional life. The benefits are endless. You will have more focus, more energy, greater health, and improved finances as these align you with your goals and minimise distractions.

1. Begin each day with a grateful heart. Recall 3 things that you are grateful for. This will align you with your Higher-Self and core values.

2. Set your intention for the day. Ask yourself, "What is my intention for today?"

3. Visualise your day. Take a few moments and imagine your day flowing, taking inspired action, and living on purpose.

4. Take inspired action. When you feel inspired, this is the perfect time to take action. We can journal and visualise a purpose-filled life, however we also need to take action towards it.

5. Declutter. This will help to minimise distractions that may pop up throughout your day.

6. Schedule. What gets scheduled, gets done. Allow time for things that light you up and that align with your intention and purpose. It is easy to get distracted by social media and endlessly scrolling; however, this can drain your energy and shift you away from your intention.

Meditate for a few moments and ask yourself, "What is my intention for today?" Allow what wants to flow through and write it in the space below or your beloved journal. Be specific. You could be focused on your health, taking inspired action, or finding joy throughout your day. Whatever you intention for the day is, be specific.

What is my intention for today?

Now ask, "What actions can I take towards this intention today?" This will enable you to remain focused on your intention and take value-based action.

Take a few moments now to visualise your day, living with your intention, and allow that to be your guiding light.

"Abracadabra. I create as I speak"

HEBREW PROVERB

8
The Universe Is Constantly Responding To You

The Power Of Words

WORDS have POWER!

Words cast spells.

That is why it's called spelling.

As we have already noted, the word 'abracadabra' in ancient Aramaic or Hebrew when translated means, "I will create as I speak."

We are learning how we are constantly creating our reality, consciously or unconsciously.

A good indication of what your subconscious thoughts are is to look around you. Whatever you see and feel you have created, consciously or unconsciously.

So we may as well create what we want, rather than what we don't want.

The quality of your life is directly influenced by the quality of your words, phrased into questions.

We are responsible for everything that shows up in our life. Every experience, every person, every situation – everything! That simple awareness can be activating.

We can either choose to feel empowered or dis-empowered by that revelation.

I choose empowered.

Returning to Maya Angelou, "When you know better, do better." This directly influences the quality of our questions.

Most people ask, "What is wrong with me?" or "Why me – why do bad things always happen to me?" And so it continues down the path of blame and shame, which keeps us stuck in victim consciousness.

Remember, the Universe responds to your questions, your frequency, and your vibration. By asking these types of questions, the Universe responds by showing you more of what you are asking.

Our conscious awareness influences the quality of our questions, so it's vital that we consider asking ourselves better questions and what they may be. We grow in two ways, either through pain or through insight, kenshō versus satori.

Kenshō Versus Satori

The difference between growing through pain or growing through insight sounds simple enough; however, when presented with these two concepts, we feel we may always choose insight. Who would consciously want to choose pain, right?

Though the truth is, we dance through both of these throughout our life. They are designed to help us evolve and grow through our human experience.

As you read through the following definitions, reflect on your life and see how you have recently been growing, through either pain (kenshō) or insight (satori)?

Kenshō

Kenshō is growth through pain.

Pain enters our life to prompt us to make a shift. Pain often means we are trying to find satisfaction in the same space we are being pushed to grow, led by ego. If you feel stagnant, blocked, and pushed, then you remain the same; there is no growth or expansion. This is the same as trying to heal in the same place you got sick.

Growth through pain is slow and gradual. We often don't witness the growth through the process; however, when we come through it at the other end and self-reflect, we see we have in fact grown.

If you look back to three years ago versus where you are now, I am willing to bet that you are a completely different person if you have chosen to grow through the awareness brought on by kenshō. If nothing has changed to three years ago, and you are in fact the same person, than I am also willing to bet you are feeling pain, dis-comfort and dis-ease in your life.

Satori

Satori is growth through insight.

This is by far a more pleasurable way to experience growth, but it occurs less often. This is growth through a sudden awakening. It's an "aha" moment that you feel, the light-bulb goes on, and it's instant.

Both kenshō and satori are great teachers. It is the gift of insight that comes from growth and expansion. Remember, the Universe is progressive and constantly expanding. By embracing change and transformation, we are aligning with the Universe and following our soul-mission.

When you next experience a painful moment, kenshō, the invitation is to ask the question, "What can I learn from this pain to help make me grow?" Adopt the lessons learned from this experience, embrace the insight, and witness your soul's expansion.

I invite you to shift attention away from dwelling on painful circumstances and begin healing by asking meaningful questions. By asking 'why' something happened or "Why does this always happen to me?" the Universe shows you more of that. Reprogramme your mind to find the good in every situation and switch to more empowering questions. You will have an opportunity to reflect further on this in *SacredPlay*.

Briefly, some examples of empowering questions are:

- What is seeking to emerge through me?
- What good is here that I presently cannot see?

- What gifts do I have that are ready to bloom?

Remember, the Universe is ALWAYS responding to your questions. The Universe is always saying "YES" to you. So be sure to ask empowering questions. You do not get what you want, you get what you are interested in.

An example of this: if you are constantly talking about lack, debt, and scarcity, yet, at the same time, asking the Universe for more money, then you are going to attract more debt, worry, lack, scarcity, etc.

We talk to ourselves all day, every day. It is important to catch the thoughts and beliefs that are dis-empowering us or keeping us in victim mode and shift it towards a more empowering thought and belief. This takes daily practice.

We are moving through shifting ancestral patterns and beliefs. We have a choice whether we want to go beyond and reprogramme our genes. Our thoughts and beliefs have the power to change our DNA; this has been proven by epigenetics. Isn't that enough incentive to want to set up a more empowering belief system and thought program?

Sweet Surrender

Oh, sweet surrender, powerful, Divine flow. What does surrender mean? Firstly, it is not acquiescing; we are not 'giving up'.

Surrender involves a deep trust in the Universe. It is allowing what is intended to flow through you and into your life. We simply yield to it. We are surrendering to what is deep within us and that which wishes to express itself through us.

When we surrender the physical control or safety net that is caging us, and say yes to the Universe and trust what wants to flow to and through us, we are aligning ourselves to our soul's purpose and embodying our sovereignty.

We are letting go of the 'how' something flows to us, being patient, and allowing it to unfold for us, orchestrated by the Universe in Divine timing.

Relinquishing control to the Universe gives us a sense of freedom. We are not forcing, pushing, or going against the grain; we are flowing with the current, like a rivercraft down the stream.

Some examples of empowering affirmations to help you to practice surrender are:

- I surrender to the Divine and know that it is the source of all my good.
- I surrender to more joy than I have ever imagined.
- I surrender to what is seeking to emerge through me.
- I let go of control and allow the Universe to guide me.
- I let go of how this is going to come to me and I am open to receiving.

All spiritual growth and unfoldment is about letting go of our perceived limitations. Are you willing to let go of your story? A deep awareness of self allows us to move beyond the victim stage and frees us from shame, blame, guilt, fear, scarcity, and rather move towards embodying our sovereignty, embracing, and celebrating our human experience.

When we truly know ourselves, we have a deep sense of self-worth and love that paves the way for worthiness. When we know and love ourselves unconditionally, we see clearly and feel compelled to take inspired action towards our soul's purpose.

Surrender is a word of empowerment. It is a sense of deep humility. We are offering ourselves up to life and what wants to be expressed through us, through our gifts, talents, and soul purpose. This can be challenging to our 'ego'.

The 'ego' is simply a sense of self. When it is balanced, it serves us. The ego operates from the limbic mind, the reptilian brain, and is based on instinct; it's programmed and designed to keep you safe. It does not like change and resists expansion and growth.

When we are coming from a place of ego, everything is "me", "mine", or "my"'. How often do you say those three words in a day? How does your ego show up and try to take credit for all the things you are doing? This comes from a place of control and fear.

We do not want to allow our ego to dominate our lives. By dissolving the ego, we transcend it and live from a higher source.

As we transcend the ego and activate our intuition and listen to the whispers of our soul, we begin to have a sense of unity with all. We feel love, compassion, and we think from a higher source and order of being.

By moving away from fear and scarcity, we embrace excitement and enthusiasm. We do this with courage and through affirmations and meditation.

No Complaints

We have brought much awareness to our words, our thoughts, our actions, and our emotions. Now I invite you to go a whole day without complaining, without having a single negative thought, or saying a negative word. One single day. 24 hours.

It sounds simple enough; however, this conscious practice will quickly show how often a negative thought, feeling, emotion, or even a word is expressed through us. This is our ego attempting to control us and keep us small.

This is a powerful way to align with your intention, Higher-Self, and the Universe. As an infinite spiritual being, it is our nature to express graciousness, flow, abundance, and love. We are returning to this state and bringing Heaven on Earth.

Remember, your words cast spells; you are telling the Universe what you want with every thought and word, placing an order, so to speak. So be mindful of the words you use.

When you find yourself having a negative thought or saying something negative, quickly replace it with a positive affirmation. I immediately cancel the negative thought in my mind; I may even say out loud to cancel the thought in order to instantly replace it with a more positive, uplifting expression – one that will serve me and draw in growth and expansion.

Go to sleep each night with the vibration of health, joy, peace, love and vibration in your heart, and visualise your dream life. Journal how this looks and feels for you.

The Power Of Yes

The power of saying YES when it serves your greatest good is in full alignment with your infinite spiritual being and dharma. Saying yes can be the difference between living your life on purpose or living someone else's life.

By saying yes, we are inadvertently saying no to what doesn't serve us. By saying yes to opportunities and designing our life, we are saying yes to living an extraordinary life, and saying no to living an ordinary life.

What have you said yes to, either consciously or unconsciously? By focusing on what we want and saying yes to it, we achieve a more desired outcome in life. In fact, life gets better and better. Some ways saying yes benefits our life is listed below:

- We experience more abundance in all areas of our life: mentally, emotionally, physically, spiritually, and financially.
- We attract more soulful, harmonious relationships.
- Our Body Temple thrives with greater health and wellness.
- We enjoy a better lifestyle by making better choices.
- We attract more money.
- We experience more fun and adventure.

- We are open to greater possibilities.
- We are open to more opportunities.
- We experience giving and receiving love in all areas of our life,
- And this is just to list a few!

So how do you choose to live? On purpose? Or by default? Say YES to what turns you on, to living a life on purpose, to being of service to others, and saying NO to an ordinary, mundane life.

Sacred Play

Meditate and ask yourself the following questions – remember without judgement – simply witness and reflect. Journal your responses below or in your companion journal.

Where do I feel stuck or pushed in my life?

Reflect on a situation or circumstance that you may have found yourself being challenged. Ask yourself the question, "If this situation were to last forever, what quality would I have to develop to bring peace into my life? How can I find my bliss in this situation?" Allow yourself to reflect and see what emerges in response to these questions.

Take a few moments and reflect on a situation, painful circumstance, or outcome where you may have felt disempowered and look for the silver-lining. See what emerges.

What good is here that I presently cannot see? Seek the insight through the pain.

What gifts do I have within that are ready to bloom?

Bring self-awareness as you move throughout your day and notice how often you may say, "me", "mine", or "my". Witness how your ego may show up and try to take credit for all the things you are doing. Write these down, without judgement, in your beloved journal or the space provided below. This consciousness and compassion will allow you to transcend your ego.

Please note that taking credit when credit is due is a form of self-love, however we don't wish to be overly boastful or always blowing our own trumpet to make ourselves feel good or to fill an internal or emotional void.

How often do I try to take credit for things I or others have done?

Create some powerful affirmations to help you surrender and fully place your trust in the Universe. Incorporate these into your daily practice. Some examples are below:

"I am safe and place my trust in the Divine timing of the Universe."

"The Universe always has my back and things are unfolding exactly as they need to."

"I am safe and supported by the Universe."

What does it look and feel like to live a life filled with health, joy, bliss, and harmony?

Ask yourself how you can surrender more to the Universe. Journal some ways below.

What does surrender feel and look like for me?

"Ego says, 'Once everything falls into place, I'll feel peace.' Spirit says 'Find your peace, and then everything will fall into place.'"

MARIANNE WILLIAMSON

9
Universal Laws And Spiritual Principles

Universal Laws And Spiritual Principles Of The Universe

The Universe is orderly and is made up of many principles and laws. These are the same principles that govern all creation, the same principles that nature embodies and creates everything we see, hear, smell, taste, and touch.

No doubt you have heard of some of these laws; for example, the Law of Karma (Cause and Effect), the Law of Attraction and Manifestation, the Law of Circulation, and the Law of Dharma, to name a few. More of the laws and principles are listed further down below, along with a brief description of each and how these can be applied to your life.

Once you understand these laws and incorporate them into your consciousness and daily life, you will then have the ability to navigate the human experience more smoothly, with a greater sense of playfulness. You'll be more open and loving and have the ability to manifest anything you desire and create a fulfilled and abundant life.

Our purpose as a spiritual being having a human experience is to act in accordance with the laws of the universe and nature. Everything in nature grows masterfully and in Divine timing. There is no force or wilful push; you do not see nature 'trying to grow', or forcing a flower to bloom: it all occurs with ease and flow.

Our human 'ego' often forces us to push, forcing our way to achieve an objective. We have a belief system that we have to work hard to achieve anything in life. However, this is not so.

I am inviting you to develop a more spiritual approach to how you are creating your life that is more in line with your natural state of being. In spiritual terms, our success is measured by how effortlessly and seamlessly we co-create with the Universe. The Universe contains your pure potential and resides within it, all the source of all your power.

By gaining an understanding of these laws and principles and by connecting with the Universe, our success is inevitable.

Let us first establish where you may be a 'willing' participant in life – aligning with the universal laws and principles – or where you may be 'wilful'?

'Wilful' means we are forcing. We are attempting to force our will and control how things come into our life.

'Willing' means we are open to receiving and allowing life to flow to us. We are 'willing' our intentions to come into our life and not attempting to force our will.

By setting an intention, we are setting the vibration and direction for our life.

We want to be willingly open to giving and receiving what flows through us. Many attempt to impose their will and be 'wilful', by forcing or controlling how their intentions or desires are to manifest into their life. Being 'wilful' or by attempting to control or force how things manifest into your life is based with the 'ego'. It involves a sense of fear and comes from a deep wound within us. By attempting to force and control how our desires are manifested, we are actually blocking them.

When you want to draw things into your life and manifest your desires, match the vibration and frequency of them and allow them to flow to you willingly. The Universe will always match your frequency and vibration and respond to this.

The Universe is progressive and constantly expanding. We are connected to the infinite Universe, and this also causes us to expand, hence growth is our infinite nature. We learned earlier how our growth comes in two ways, pain or insight, either through kenshō or satori. How we grow is up to us.

Spiritual Laws Of The Universe

There are many spiritual laws of the Universe. The Universe is constantly expanding and growing, so must we be. By aligning ourselves to the spiritual laws of the Universe, we are aligning with our Higher-Self and higher power. That, in itself, is transformative, and by living in alignment, enables you to co-create with the Universe.

Below are 7 spiritual laws of the Universe and how you can align with them. These spiritual laws and principles are designed to help you embody your true nature of growth and expansion and co-create with the Universe. There are many more laws and principles; however, I have listed my top 7 to help you to navigate this Earthly experience with ease and flow as a Divine spiritual being.

The Law Of Pure Potential

The Law of Pure Potential is the source of all our creativity and possibilities. It is pure consciousness. It is knowing our true nature, our true Self, and also knowing that anything is possible. One way to experience this is through meditation. Through our quiet meditation and mind, we are able to receive the vision of our pure potential.

Quieten the mind, connect with infinite oneness, and experience the innate potential that exists within you and is surrounding you. This truly acts as an awakening, an activating and expansive experience, reconnecting with your true self and nature. When sitting in meditation, remember to simply witness what emerges and practice non-judgement.

Another way is spending time in nature. Nature continuously demonstrates infinite potential and possibilities. She flourishes through adversity and thrives against all odds. Nature's ability to regenerate and grow is pure potential. The continuous cycle of death and rebirth demonstrates that anything is possible.

Consider a way that you can spend more time in nature to gain this sense of potential.

The Law Of Giving And Receiving

The Law of Giving and Receiving is simple; what you wish to receive, you give. The intention behind our giving and receiving is the most important thing. If you give with an expectation of return, that creates imbalance and stagnates energy. Nor can you hold on to something – for example, money.

If you attempt to hold onto money, to hoard it from a sense of lack or scarcity, then that stops the flow and circulation. Reflect on your breath for a moment. You cannot simply breathe out all the time (giving), nor attempt to breathe in constantly (receiving): there is an equal breath in and out. This simply demonstrates the law of circulation, giving and receiving.

When the intention behind the giving is joyful, without expectation, the energy behind the giving raises exponentially. Always give with a joyful heart. The more you give, the more you receive. If you want love, give love. If you want to be blessed with more good things in life, then silently bless others for all the things that show up in their lives. Be happy for them and show appreciation. Silently wish everyone joy, peace, love, and abundance. The Universe will reward you in countless ways.

It is important to also gracefully accept all gifts that life offers you. These are coming from your Higher-Self and the Universe through others. These can be delivered as a compliment, a kind word, an offer from a friend to make you a meal, someone buying you a coffee, or being given a gift. Be open to receiving all. The Universe loves a grateful heart and will give you more to be grateful for.

The Law Of Circulation

Everything is energy. Love is energy. Money is energy. E-motion is 'energy in motion'. The Law of Circulation shows us that energy is constantly flowing, and if money is energy, that, too, is constantly flowing. When something is 'spent', it is gone, no longer is it in circulation: it disappears. Now, think about that in relation to energy and money.

When you are out shopping or making a purchase, what would you normally say? "I just 'spent' some money?" Poof! It is gone, never to return. Now, with that conscious awareness, I want you to start thinking that each time you purchase something or exchange money, think about 'circulating' money, not 'spending' it. Then law dictates that it must come back.

Each time I purchase something I say to myself, "Plenty more where that came from," or, "I'm circulating money, and it will come back to me 1,000 times or more." These are more empowering and affirming statements, and they align with the Law of Circulation and the Law of Attraction.

Now, it is not all about receiving, which is what The Secret or other law of attraction teachers may speak about. We do not want to overly focus on the take, take, take. We also must give in order to receive.

Giving and receiving is a complete cycle. Just like the cycle of our breath. In order for it to be complete, we must take an in-breath and an out-breath. We give and receive air. This completes the cycle and circulation.

In order to receive, we must surrender to the Universe and open ourselves to more good than we have ever imagined. Remember, we get what we focus on. A belief is a focused thought.

Everything we receive, every gift, is from the Universe. Next time someone buys you a coffee or gives you a gift, consider this is a gift directly from Source. It is coming through a fellow human being to deliver it to you. Graciously receive all gifts from the Universe.

When someone gives you a compliment, say thank you. This is a form of a gift and a way to practice receiving.

Our capacity to receive is directly linked to our capacity to give. If you are wanting love, then give love. If you are wanting more money, then give money, fully trusting and surrendering to the Universe that it will provide for you. However, we must remember to give without expectation of return, otherwise this is not truly giving. Only give with a full heart and it will return to you in abundance.

I hear you saying, "But I don't have any money, that's why I want more. I can't give away what I don't have." This is coming from a place of scarcity and lack. Remember, money is energy. When you are circulating money, know that it will return to you in the same feeling that you are giving, so be mindful of your giving. This can be applied when you are paying rent, mortgage, food, bills, etc. When you do give, do so with a generous heart, feel full and abundant, and this will return to you exponentially.

However, if we give from a place of scarcity, from fear or lack, then we are only going to attract more fear and lack.

At a higher level of consciousness, we only get to keep what we give away. When we are feeling full and generous, then the Universe will provide more things for us to feel full and generous about.

This is a deep spiritual teaching. When we think about giving and act on that thought, the Universe will then provide more for us to give.

You are the creator of your reality. We are all creators; however, we are moving towards being more gracious 'soul creators'. We no longer simply want a bigger boat, a new car, or material possessions – just to keep up with the neighbours – or the latest toy or handbag to fill a hole in our heart. When we are attempting to fill a void in our heart or emotions with material possessions, it will never be enough. That void can never be filled by such things.

At one time or another, you may have made a purchase when you were feeling low, and soon thereafter felt buyer's remorse. This comes from seeking gratification, a quick fix from external sources. We do not want to feel or delve into our emotions and uncover why we are feeling a certain way, so we made a purchase on a whim, only to regret it later.

That is why we must practice deep introspection and develop self-mastery. When we know ourselves, self-reflect, and have self-awareness, we are taking responsibility for our emotions, our actions, and our choices, and we are being self-disciplined.

Give without expectation of return. Give with a full and gracious heart and the Universe will give you more to give.

Abundance is seeking to express itself through you, as you. Abundance is your birthright. When we are tapping into the whispers of our soul and actively listening to what wishes it wants to express through us, we are making something welcome.

When we relinquish control of the 'how' something is supposed to come into our life, we become available to what wants to emerge. We receive inspiration and are moved towards inspired action. When we let go of control and surrender to the flow of life and Universe through our affirmations and visualisations, we then allow what is ready to emerge through us.

Practice graciousness when receiving. Many of us may find it difficult to receive, even if it's just a compliment. This is directly linked to our self-worth. Remember, all gifts come from the Universe. When we turn down a gift or are being ungrateful, we are actually turning down the Universe. You are pushing your manifestations further away rather than drawing them closer.

Practice giving and receiving and see how your world begins to transform positively.

Sacred Play

Ground and meditate for a few minutes and work through the following insights:

Look through the life structures below and reflect on what areas of your life where you feel you are a 'master manifestor' and which ones may need some focus. Use the space below to record your findings or grab your faithful journal and write what flows through you.

Next, write an empowering question and affirmation for each life structure that requires greater focus. This will enable greater receptivity and more gracious giving.

> **What empowering questions and affirmations can I use for my life structures to allow greater giving and receiving?**
>
> **Spiritual**

Ego

Livelihood

Body Temple

Beliefs

Relationships

Money / Finances

Community

Create your own empowering affirmation for when making purchases or circulating money, and write it below. For example, "There is plenty more where that came from."

Always look to ways you can give and feel generous. Ask yourself, "How can I give today?" and the Universe will provide more for you, in order for you, in turn, to give. For example, "I am going to give a smile to everyone I make eye contact with today."

Ask yourself, "How can I be more open to receiving?" – whether that be compliments, gifts, etc. Write down your findings below and bring conscious awareness to your day to be more receptive. For example, "I will graciously say thank you to all the gifts the Universe gives to me today."

The Law Of Cause And Effect Or Karma

Everyone has heard the term "What goes around, comes around" or "You reap what you sow." The Law of Karma is not one to be feared, as it also holds positive outcomes. If you want happiness, then plant seeds of happiness wherever you go. It simply states that for every action, there is a reaction – a cause and effect.

It is about having a conscious awareness regarding your decision-making. A lot of our choices are made unconsciously; therefore, we often feel we do not have a choice. This may be a result of conditioning.

The more awareness and consciousness you bring to your life and to your choices, and then bring the decision into your heart-space, our intuitive centre, the more aligned we will be with the Universe, and the less fearful we will be of the Law of Karma.

Whenever you make a choice, feel into your heart-space and ask yourself these questions:

- What are the consequences of this choice?
- Will this choice bring happiness to all involved?

If you are experiencing the karmic effect of a decision you have already made, learn to look for the silver lining, the golden opportunity to learn and grow from this lesson. This will help transform and transcend the choice into evolutionary success. The sooner you are able to see the lesson or blessing, the sooner you are able to transcend the choice.

The Law Of Least Effort

This spiritual law invites us to look to nature, where everything functions from infinite intelligence with effortlessness, ease, flow, harmony, and love. The principle of "set it and forget it" applies here. You have set your intention, asked the Universe, aligned with your Higher-Self, and raised your frequency and vibration: the law of least effort will now deliver your desires, effortlessly.

When our actions are motivated by inspired action and love, our energy abounds and seems effortless. The Law of Least Effort invites you to flow with the Universe and to stop resisting or forcing. This law invites us to surrender to the Divine and allow things to evolve in their natural state of flow.

By achieving self-mastery, living authentically, incorporating self-reflection, self-discipline, self-responsibility, and self-awareness into our lives, we simply stop fighting and resisting, and we can be fully present in life. We are able to capture our vision, take inspired action, and allow life to flow with effortless ease.

The Law Of Detachment

The Law of Detachment invites us to relinquish control and surrender to the Universe. It is sweet surrender.

We could say the opposite of surrender is attachment, which inherently implies mistrust and doubt. We are attempting to control how things come to us, which is based in fear. We can still set our intentions and desires; however, we may need to relinquish the way in which it materialises in our life.

Let me be clear, this is not a matter of simply acquiescing or just giving up. We are surrendering to the Universe, which sees all the infinite potential and possibilities for the way in which something can be delivered to us. Detachment allows pure creativity and freedom to emerge, and opportunities arise in alignment with our Higher-Self and the Universe. More on attachment, detachment, and non-attachment later in this handbook.

Remember, you are an infinite spiritual being having a human experience. What would the infinite expansive Universe give unto itself? Everything. Surrender to the Universe; allow it to deliver to you more abundance than you have ever imagined.

The Law Of Attraction And Manifestation

The Law of Attraction or Manifestation became renowned through the movie, The Secret. This is also the second state of our conscious awareness: the manifesting stage.

Remember, the first state was victim consciousness, where we feel we have no control of what is happening in our life, and we are seeking to blame outside of ourselves. The second state, the manifesting stage, is where we begin to consciously create and manifest our dreams and goals.

The Law of Attraction and Manifestation follows the concept of consciously creating your reality, manifesting your desires and intentions, and materialising them into the physical realm. It is the concept that our thoughts create our reality. By mastering our ability to manifest, we are enabled to have fun and play with our life. We are creating our reality in every moment, so we may as well have some fun along the way!

This is an extremely fun part of our human experience whilst on this Earth. I invite you to play with it.

If you do not have everything you desire in your life, then there is a block or conflicting story in your subconscious, a held belief that counteracts what you desire. For example, if you have been trying to manifest money and wealth into your life, and it starts to flow in but you are unable to keep it – unforeseen bills pop up or you need to pay for something unexpected – then our money flows out again. This means there is a deep-seated belief within you that conflicts your abundance story.

A hidden belief is what we are manifesting: our subconscious mind is holding onto this belief system and this is where our programming is being played. We need to uncover this resistance or block, realise the habit-forming belief and create a new belief through higher-habits so that we can live an abundant and fulfilled life, knowing it is your birthright.

By using the Law of Attraction, we are taking back our mind and imagination. Use this law as a tool to reprogramme disempowering beliefs and emotions. It is time to get creative and have fun!

Remember that our thoughts create our emotions; we act from our emotions, and this creates our reality. The words we speak to ourselves and others are important.

There are a few simple steps you can follow:

1. **Meditate.** Ground yourself; take a few deep breaths to centre and meditate for a few minutes.

2. **Visualise.** Focus on what you want to create or draw into your life. Spend some time visualising your goals and dreams. Visualise it as if you are living it in the present moment. You are living your dream life now! This is the Law of Pure Potential.

3. **Feel.** Get emotional about what you want. How does it feel to be living your dream life? The money, car, home, love, friendships, community, holiday – all the things you desire in your life. Feel the bliss, joy, happiness, peace, and freedom that comes with living your dream life.

4. **Release.** Release your intentions and desires to the Universe without expectation of how they will manifest and materialise back into your life. This is an important step. Set your intention and then release it, forget it. Remember, this is the Law of Detachment.

5. **Allow.** Go about your day and week and let the Universe deliver in Divine timing, in its own unique way, all the things you desire to you. Do not get caught up in the details. This is the Law of Least Effort; simply surrender and allow flow.

It is important to stay high-vibe and positive about your manifestations. Spend each day visualising your dream life. Feel it as if you are living it and the Universe will deliver. Be sure to follow your intuition and guidance. This is how the Universe speaks to us. Take inspired action in manifesting your dreams; however, remember to release control where necessary. Be sure you are ready and open to receive your manifestations.

The Law Of Dharma

Dharma is the principle that governs the Universe. For you to live out your dharma means to live in accordance with the Universe. It is living in accordance with the grand plan for humanity. We are all spiritual beings, having a human experience, and the Law of Dharma expresses our physical expression or purpose in this lifetime. The Law of Dharma is your soul purpose.

Every being has a purpose to fulfil in this lifetime, a unique gift or talent that is waiting to be expressed through them. It is no accident that you are here. You have chosen to come to this Earth, in this lifetime, to have an Earthly experience.

Your fingerprint demonstrates your uniqueness. There is only one of you on this entire Earth of all the millions of beings who walked before you. That is not a mistake – you Divinely orchestrated your arrival on this Earth, and it is time to unleash your pure potential and live your dharma.

The Law of Dharma implies your unique destiny, your purpose in life. When we discover this purpose and express this gift by being of service to others, we are living our life purpose or in accordance with dharma.

How do we find our dharma or life purpose?

- **Firstly,** you are here to discover your true Self and your Divinity, to remember you are an infinite spiritual being and reconnect with your Higher-Self and the Universe.
- **Secondly,** you are here to uncover your unique talent or gift that you are here to express. Your gift is unique to you, a talent that can only be expressed through you.
- **Thirdly,** your purpose in life is to use your unique gift or talent and be in service to others.

By reconnecting with your Higher-Self, uncovering your unique gift or talent, and expressing that gift by being of service to others, abundance flows. You experience true joy and the true meaning of success in life. There is a *SacredPlay* activity later for you to complete to help you uncover your dharma and soul expression.

By aligning ourselves to the spiritual laws and principles of the Universe, we are living in full alignment and co-creating with our Higher-Self and the Universe. We begin embracing and rejoicing our human experience, which brings harmony and ease.

Sacred Play

Meditate upon the Universal Principles and Spiritual Laws and reflect where you may have been either a 'willing' or 'wilful' participant.

Ask yourself the following questions and write down your responses in the spaces provided below or your beloved journal.

Where in my life am I showing my pure potential? (The Law of Pure Potential)

Where in my life can I willingly give more? (The Law of Giving and Receiving and Circulation)

Do I graciously accept and receive gifts the Universe is offering me? (The Law of Least Effort)

Reflect on some of the decisions you have made and ask yourself, "What is the lesson I can learn from this experience?" (The Law of Cause and Effect or Karma)

What am I consciously creating and materialising? (The Law of Attraction and Manifesting).

"The meaning of life is to find your gift. The purpose of life is to give it away."

PABLO PICASSO

10
Uncover Your Unique Soul Expression And Dharma

What Is Your Soul Expression And Dharma?

Your gifts are a unique expression of your talent, your soul's expression that only you possess. Some consider it their 'purpose'. This is the higher truth that answers all our questions about who we are, why we are here, and what we are here to do. Many ask, "How do I uncover my purpose?"

Your purpose in this lifetime is to remember your Divinity, your unique gifts, and express your talents and share these with others.

Living your dharma, uncovering your soul's purpose (your 'why'), leads to remembering 'who you are'.

Once you establish your unique gifts and expression of these talents, you begin to feel compelled to take action, to be of service to others – because not doing so will cause more pain than following your purpose.

This allows you to live in full alignment with your soul and to surrender to your purpose. This is living your dharma.

Living with purpose is also living 'purposefully'. Being in the moment, living consciously, and developing self-mastery. This is how we unfold what is seeking to emerge through us from within us. Being in the moment, fully present, enables us to capture our vision for our lives.

Allow yourself to be guided by your vision, and let it lead you into taking inspired action. Take time daily to meditate and give space for your visions to come through. Think back and consider, what did you love to do as a child? What lights you up? These can often lead to your dharma.

If you have yet to uncover your unique gifts and talents, or have not yet established your life purpose, then create an intention or quality that you would like to live by.

For example, you may like to live a more peaceful, joyful, happy, loving, blissful existence. Pick a quality and set that intention to live life by, and your soul purpose will begin to unfold. You will be compelled into action.

It is important to integrate your insights so that you can embody them. This invites transformation into your life and true soul embodiment and mastery. Work through the *SacredPlay* to enable your transformation and help you uncover your gifts and unique talents, your purpose, and your 'why'.

What Is My Why?

It is important to understand 'why' you do what you do. We are navigating towards self-mastery, to live in harmony with the laws of the Universe and our dharma.

Your 'why' is deep-seated within you; it is not simply because it is what others are doing or to 'make money'. That is an egoistic response, and we are moving into a more conscious way of being. We are moving towards your unique soul expression and living your dharma.

Sacred Play

We are going to establish what is seeking to emerge through you and what is ready to bloom.

Sit quietly, take some deep breaths and meditate for a few moments. Reflect on the following questions and journal your answers. Remember, we want to uncover your unique gifts and talents, your soul purpose – not mimic what others are doing.

When considering the following questions, write down the first thing that comes to mind. Don't ruminate over the answers; don't overthink, as this can then involve the ego. You may also begin to contemplate what is expected or what you 'think you should do' rather than acknowledge what truly wants to emerge from your soul's expression.

The intention is to uncover your hidden talents, desires, and dharma, so it's vital to focus on what comes into your head first.

Consider, if money were of no concern and you had all the time in the world, what would you do? How would you utilise your days?

Complete the *SacredPlay* below, whilst considering the above:

What did I love to do as a child, that lights me up?

Make a list of your unique talents. These are your gifts and often come naturally to you.

How do you express your gifts? List all the things that you love to do with your unique gifts and talents.

How may I be of service to others? How can I help? How can I serve others in my community?

What skills do I love to apply or want to get better at?

What lights me up now?

What do I love to research in my spare time or for fun?

Where does my mind go when I have free time? What do I find myself day-dreaming about?

What do I know a lot about?

How can I unleash the potential that is within me?

It is often said that our wound is our gift. If you find a wound, you find your worth. In fact, many 'become' the very person, guide, or mentor they themselves needed when they were younger or in their hour of need.

If you find uncovering your unique gifts and talents challenging, then create an intention or quality that you would like to live by. For example, you may like to set the intention to pursue happiness.

What intention would I like to live life by?

Now reflect on your responses above and contemplate the following questions. Keep asking yourself 'why?' after each answer. Be childlike in questioning yourself. Take your time and remember to be completely honest with yourself. No one else needs to read your responses. This is solely for you.

Why do I want to do this?

Why do I feel like I want to do it?

What do I think I will get out of it?

What do I want to get out of it?

"Remember, love is not attachment, love knows no attachment, and that which knows attachment is not love. That is possessiveness, domination, clinging, fear, greed — it may be a thousand and one things, but it is not love."

OSHO

11
Attachment, Non-Attachment And Detachment

What Is The Difference Between Attachment, Non-Attachment And Detachment?

The concepts of attachment, non-attachment, and detachment stems from Buddhist teachings. Understanding these concepts and how they apply in our daily life is an important part for us to navigate this Earthly experience with ease and flow.

Attachment

Attachment is when we place an emotional charge on things, a person, or an outcome. We have an expectation of how things should be and are attached to them. We may be linking our survival to it. This could be a lifestyle, a job, our phone or device, a person, a title, our public image, something or someone where we feel we simply cannot live without it or them. It's as if our happiness or abundance depends on it.

This is stemmed from seeking outside of ourselves to fill a void within. Attaching our joy and abundance to things outside of us, seeking external validation, or relying on others to make us happy can never be truly long-lasting, genuine, or stable.

When we want certain things and attempt to control the outcome, we can often feel frustrated. The moment the thing or person is removed, or the outcome we expected falls short, our abundance or happiness is also gone, which is why it is an impossible void to fill.

When we understand that only we can have full mastery over our experience, that we are creators of our reality, and the only true source to all our happiness comes from living in full alignment, not from an ego-based external source, then we can be one with our Higher-Self. Our Higher-Self knows that true security, happiness, and abundance comes from within.

Non-Attachment

Non-attachment is when we are fully available, fully participating in life, in our journey, and in our experiences; however, we are not attached to the outcome. We are living in the present moment and we remain conscious of our thoughts and actions.

We understand that we are the creators of our reality and what we think is what we become. Being non-attached enables us to go and do our very best, allowing what flows through us to unfold. It also enables more good than we ever imagined to flow to us. Often, we are limiting our own abundance by being attached to a specific outcome. Whenever I am journalling or scripting, I always add, "If not this, then something better." This aligns with the Universal truth, knowing that I am always supported by the Universe. It knows a greater plan than what I can see from my human point of view.

This is not about constantly seeking the next best thing; that, again, is based on attachment to external things for validation. This is about aligning with the Universe and flowing with our intuition and guidance from our Higher-Self.

Holding onto something is also coming from a place of scarcity. If we hold on too tightly, we are sending a message to the Universe saying that there is only one of this 'thing' and we believe that it is limited in resources or that we cannot receive more. This may be in the form of money, people, jobs, places, and even emotions, which can lead to feeling stuck, anxious, or frustrated.

By releasing attachment and living in non-attachment, we are sending a sign to the Universe that we are open to greater opportunities and we welcome abundance, joy, peace, and happiness into our lives. We are open to more good than we ever imagined possible.

Detachment

This is vastly different to non-attachment. Detachment is lethargy, not caring, despondency, and a general sense of wanting to detach from life due to a pain point.

Detachment resembles a lack of love or compassion. This can lead us to distancing ourselves from the world, feeling wounded, uncaring, isolated, indifferent, and even disconnected from ourselves and our emotions. In this sense, we are not fully engaging in our life. This goes against our inner being, ignoring that we are infinite spiritual beings sourced from Love.

Everything we seek is readily available within us. When we are living in alignment, and have gained self-mastery, there is no need to seek things externally, and we have no attachment to things, people, or outcomes. We know that we are powerful, spiritual beings, everything flows to us with grace and ease in Divine timing. We are no longer attached to an outcome; we are living in non-attachment.

We experience greater outcomes in life when we are not attached. Being a full and willing participant in our journey guarantees a fulfilled, happy, and abundant experience. This is living with Universal alignment.

Sacred Play

Reflect on your life experiences and where you may be holding onto attachment or feeling detached. This is not an exercise in shaming or blaming, simply witness what comes up and write it below or in your beloved journal.

Attachment, Non-Attachment And Detachment

Where do I have some attachments in life? What do I feel my life depends on?

Where in my life have I detached myself?

Now, take a moment to celebrate areas of your life where you feel you are sitting in non-attachment and full alignment. Celebration is an important part of our human experience and it encourages us to do more of the same.

What areas of my life am I practising non-attachment?

"Intuition is a very powerful thing. More powerful than intellect."

STEVE JOBS

12
Your Intuition Is A Super Power

What Is Intuition?

Let us look at the word intuition for a moment. We can break it up into two words 'in' and 'tuition', which would refer to a learning or teaching from within, stemming from your internal, innate wisdom.

Many often describe their intuition as a deep sense of knowing, they just 'know' something to be true. Often, this is beyond logic or understanding.

A highly developed intuition is a superpower and I call it my secret weapon. Your intuition is your personal GPS. It will guide you and is always right because it is connected to Universal Source Energy.

Everyone is intuitive and we all have different ways in which we use our intuition and receive messages. Some refer to these as psychic abilities. I have listed some of the more well-known ones below. See if any resonate with you.

The name Clair is a French adjective meaning clear, hence your intuition is speaking to you in clear messages via one of the mediums below:

Top 6 Clairs:

- **Clairvoyance:** clear seeing. The ability to receive messages through images in your mind's eye.
- **Clairaudience:** clear hearing. The ability to receive messages through words and hearing phrases in your mind.
- **Clairsentience:** clear feeling. The ability to receive messages through feelings, emotions, and sensations.
- **Claircognisance:** clear knowing. The ability to receive messages as fully-formed ideas or psychic downloads.
- **Clairgustance:** clear taste. The ability to receive messages through your taste buds from things not present.
- **Clairalience:** clear smell. The ability to receive messages through smelling from things not present.

Learn and develop yours so you can listen to your internal guidance, knowing it is connected to your Higher-Self and the Universe. There are many ways you can develop and harness your intuitive abilities. Begin by journalling your thoughts and feelings, see which of the Clairs above resonate with you most.

When we notice the subtle signs and symbols we are receiving, we begin living more in harmony with our Higher-Self and amplify our co-creating with the Universe.

Visualising Versus Visioning

Visualising and visioning are vastly different; however, both have their place. Many use these terms interchangeably, but it is important to note they are different and stem from different sources: either from your 'infinite spiritual being', when we are visioning, or the 'human being', when we are visualising.

Visualising is us creating our reality through our human experience. It is using the Law of Attraction to create your life. This is an important step in your creation process to assist your ego and reptilian brain to accept change. Your brain is designed to keep you safe and does not like doing new things. This is why we always resort back to old patterns of behaviour, even when they don't serve us because, to your brain, it feels safe.

Taking time to visualise daily helps to make the unfamiliar, familiar to our brain – to visualise what life would look like and feel like living your goals and visions.

Visioning is when we are living our dharma, seeing our soul's purpose aligned with our infinite spiritual being and Higher-Self and the Universe and feeling pulled towards that reality. Our vision comes through when we are spending time in quiet meditation.

Activating our intuition allows us to receive the guidance more openly and fully from our infinite spiritual being. We want to capture this vision, articulate it, and take 'inspired action' towards that vision.

The Difference Between Ego (Instinct) And Intuition

Activating our intuition allows us to capture our vision. In order to listen to our intuition, we must first learn to differentiate between ego and intuition.

I often get asked the question, what is the difference between intuition and instinct? How do I know when it's my Higher-Self -- my human self -- or ego communicating with me?

The ego is the mind, often referred to as the monkey-mind. It is remarkably busy; it questions everything we think, say, and do, and it is very much in our head space. This is what we use the most when we are living unconsciously through life, and it often leads us to feel like life is happening to us and that we have no control. This unconscious state is the victimhood state we learned about, that everything is happening 'TO me'.

Our intuition is like a quiet, calm voice, and it comes from our heart and soul. It can feel extremely passionate and fiery too: it comes from deep within. The messages are delivered directly without question and they give you a sense of calm. Many call this their 'gut instinct' or 'gut feeling', just like a quiet sense of knowing.

The job of the mind is to secrete thoughts and we must train it, like we would any other muscle. We have full control over our mind, and we are now selecting to choose 'better thoughts'. We are consciously doing this through self-mastery, placing conscious effort to create higher-habits that serve us and ask more empowered questions that shift our behaviours and patterns.

Quietening your mind allows your visions to flow through. You can achieve this by using your breath, listening to high vibrational music, and through doing mediation. You may like to follow a guided meditation first and then spend a few quiet moments at the end to allow the visions and guidance to flow through. This takes practice, just like any new skill we are learning.

Think of it as catching up with a friend. This friend is talking nonstop, and you cannot seem to get a word in. This is the same when we are connecting with our Higher-Self and the Universe. We need to take a breath, quieten our mind, listen, and be ready to receive so that we can hear and see any messages.

Ways To Activate Your Intuition

There are many ways to activate and cultivate your intuition and I have included some exercises below for you to follow. This is by no means a definitive list and you may discover your own way of connecting and cultivating your intuition along the way or you may already have an established practice. I encourage you to try new ways as it also helps to open new pathways. Remember, this is a journey back to your infinite spiritual being, your Higher-Self, and the Universe.

- **Meditation.** Spending time daily in quiet meditation will help you connect with your Higher-Self and allow any messages, visions, and guidance to flow through you. It is important to calm the mind to be able to communicate and hear messages from the Universe, your Spirit team, and your Higher-Self.
- **Visualisation.** Take a few minutes every day to visualise what your goals and dreams look like. Visualise it as if it is happening now in your life. Feel the emotions of what it would feel like to live your dreams and visions. You may like to do this upon rising first thing in your day and before you go to sleep each night. Research shows that our

brain is most susceptible at these stages of the day, hence the benefits of visualising a life you wish to create.

- **Intentions.** For each day, set an intention for that day upon rising. You may like to use your hierarchy of values and align your intention with these. Connect with your life purpose and intentions and move throughout your day, keeping your attention on your intention.
- **Affirmations.** Recite your affirmations daily. This helps to keep you high-vibe and focused on positive energy. These can be "I AM" affirmations or other mantras. Ensure to make them positive and in the present tense. Remember, your words have power and you are casting spells: ensure they are for the highest good of all.
- **Declarations.** These are different to your intentions and affirmations. A declaration to the Universe states what you are ready to call in. For example, "I am open, ready, and available for more good in my life than I have ever imagined."
- **Breathwork.** Using your breath to calm the mind and body helps you to connect. It can also be used to go into altered states to help heal the body. You may like to start with a 4-fold breath. This is a powerful transformational breath that helps to ground you and bring you into a present state. I will guide you through this breath below.

Either sitting down with feet flat on the ground or sitting crossed legged, begin by closing your eyes. Take 3 deep breaths through your nose down into your belly and out through your mouth with a big sigh. Release the day with each breath.

Our 4-fold breath begins; inhale for a count of 4, hold for a count of 4, release for a count of 4, hold for a count of 4. Repeat this 4 times.

Return to your normal breath.

This is especially powerful when you set an intention. Your intention can be to transform an emotion you may be feeling (pain, sorrow, or grief, into joy, peace, or bliss), or you can hold an intention for your day to flow with peace and abundance.

You may choose to do this breath upon waking and/or several times throughout the day. It will only take a few minutes to complete, yet it will immediately transform your energy and day.

- **Stay high-vibe.** This is essential when we are communicating with our Higher-Self and Spirit. You cannot go in complaining and expect peace, love, and clear messages. Remember, the Universe responds to your energy, not your words. Staying high-vibe is important to receiving clear messages and visions.

- **Be present.** Avoid focusing on the past or future when connecting. This may cause anxiety and depression. Being fully present enables us to have a clearer connection and be ready to receive messages.

- **Be grateful.** The Universe loves a grateful heart. Develop an attitude of gratitude and express your deep gratitude for all the amazing things in your life. Expressing deep gratitude enhances your connection and messages. The more grateful you are, the more you will have to be grateful for.

- **Give Thanks.** Show gratitude and give thanks to your Higher-Self, Spirit Guides, and the Universe for communicating with you. The more gratitude expressed, the more they will want to continue to guide and send messages through.

- **Music.** Listen to high-vibe music. There is some great music that is 432hz (the frequency that life creates by), and above, which will heighten your connection and help keep your vibe high. Check out solfeggio playlists on YouTube or other music streaming platforms and search for high-vibe music. Incorporate this into your day and whilst you are meditating.

- **Crystals.** These beautiful semi-precious stones can help with raising your vibration and connection. Set your intention to the crystal and use them to support you. Amethyst and clear quartz are great ones to start with, but it's always best to select a crystal that you are drawn to.

- **Essential oils.** I believe essential oils are mother medicine in a bottle. They capture the divine extracts of mother nature at her finest and are available at your fingertips. When selecting essential oils, search for premium grade products as this ensures they are high-vibe and, in turn, they will help raise your vibration. Frankincense has been used for centuries in spiritual practice. Lavender is another great essential oil for connection; it also helps calm you and steadies the mind.

- **Whole food.** The food we eat and what we put in our body will reflect our connection and its clarity. Be sure to nourish yourself with whole foods and treat your body like a temple in order to allow yourself to become a conduit for the Divine. Food not only affects the body, it also impacts our mind and moods, just like the old saying, "You are what you eat." If you want to be high-vibe, then be sure to eat high-vibe food.

- **Avoid alcohol.** When 'trying to connect' with your Higher-Self and the Universe, it is best to avoid alcohol. Alcohol dulls our senses and numbs you. We are attempting to heighten your senses to be able to connect clearly and receive messages.

- **Avoid stimulants.** Again, they can cloud us and cloud our head space. We want to be clear in order to receive our visions.

- **Open your heart.** Drop into your heart space feeling open and ready to receive unconditional love. You can do this by imagine drawing green light into your heart space with your breath and feeling the love from the Universe and Spirit Team. This will enhance and heighten your connection and messages.

- **Self-Love.** This is by far the most important aspect. The more you love yourself, care for yourself, and honour and respect yourself, the more enhanced your connection with your Higher-Self and the Universe will be. You will then be able to receive, trust, and surrender to every message and guidance received.

- **Avoid Drugs.** Avoid medications where possible and any recreational drugs when developing your intuitive nature and embracing your infinite spiritual being. Drugs can impair our connection as it numbs our body, heart, mind, and soul. Yes, there are some 'drugs' and plant medicines that can be used to enhance your connection. However, it is easy to become reliant on these and you may then feel you will not be able to obtain a connection without them. We want to be able to freely connect daily and not rely on a substance to achieve that for us.

- **Reiki.** Energy healing modalities such as Reiki help clear your aura and energy and will enhance your connection. The definition or Reiki is 'life force energy', and it helps clear and balance your energy centres, also known as chakras, creating a clearer channel.
- **Keep communicating.** The more we are open to communicating and trust the messages we receive, the more vivid we will see, hear, feel, and know the messages we are receiving. Keep communicating.
- **Listen to your gut.** It will always guide you and never lead you astray.

There is no shortcut: you have to do the 'work'. It is like learning to drive a car; there are steps along the way and you require practice to become adept at it, get comfortable with your abilities, and to trust yourself.

The more you connect, the more you practice, the more enhanced your intuition and guidance will be, and therefore the 'easier' it will become. When you are first learning to activate and enhance your intuition, you also have to trust yourself, be gentle, kind, and compassionate with yourself.

Daily practice is encouraged. Intuition is like any other muscle; it requires practice to be able to 'hear', 'see', and 'feel' your messages. There are numerous ways the Universe is communicating with us, such as through signs and symbols.

You may see a random feather cross your path or it may turn up somewhere unexpected, you hear a song that just seems to talk to you, repeating numbers keep popping up throughout your day, or an animal appears seemingly out of nowhere and attracts your eye – these are all examples of how the Universe is communicating to you.

Even if you are seasoned at receiving guidance and messages, I encourage you to take inspired action on the guidance you are receiving. You may like to journal these so you can reflect on the guidance you receive and witness how it then unfolds.

Sacred Play

Spend a few minutes each day connecting and going through the intuition exercises above or any of your own that you have uncovered.

Meditate daily and journal your findings. Create a 'library' of the signs and symbols you see and what they mean to you. This will enable you to develop your intuition, enhance your connection, and increase your self-worth because you will then know what to 'look' for when receiving messages and you will learn to trust in those messages.

What are some of the signs and symbols I have received and what do they mean to me?

"Having too much of anything results in chaos, confusion, and clutter."

GERALIN THOMAS

13
The Secret Power Of Decluttering

Why Declutter?

Clutter isn't just stuff. It is anything that gets in the way of you achieving your goals.

The more we organise our physical environment, the clearer our mind and, therefore, the more we feel equipped to deal with new opportunities. If we don't stay organised, we can become overwhelmed with past tasks yet to be completed, creating a mindset of fearing the future since we are not coping with the backlog from our past.

If you have ever misplaced your keys and gone in search for them, you will understand what I mean. We can feel a sense of panic when we can't find our keys, then a sense of relief once they are found and the search is over. So I invite you to embrace the opportunity to sort, clean, and fix today: this is some of the best medicine for our soul.

Having an orderly environment is a form of self-love and your infinite being breathes a sigh of relief. It may take a little concerted effort at first to maintain some order in your environment, but remember, there is freedom in discipline. I know that may sound like an oxymoron; however, when we have created firm boundaries, established self-discipline, and are measuring self-responsibility, this demonstrates to the Universe we are creating sacred space, routines, and order. And the Universe loves order.

Having an orderly environment also creates space for new opportunities and countless possibilities. We learned earlier how the Universe is orderly, therein containing laws and principles. We are connected to the Universe via our spiritual being. It would therefore make sense for us to maintain some order in our human existence.

Start by decluttering from your physical environment. Begin with your home, working through your drawers, wardrobes, kitchen, bedroom, shed, etc. What have you been holding onto or hoarding that no longer brings you joy or serves you?

Move through your car, purse, handbag, and desk or environment at work. Keep moving through all areas of your life and aligning with your infinite spiritual being and keep clearing.

As you declutter and go through your items, a question to ask yourself is, "Does this item bring me joy?" If the answer is no or maybe, then it's time to clear it out. Will it bring another joy? Give it to good-will or donate it to a charity or someone in need. This brings us back to the law of giving and receiving and circulation.

Once you have cleared your physical environment, you will feel your mind become clearer. When you are constantly looking at clutter, subconsciously it can also clutter your mind. Your mind is constantly thinking, categorising, and prioritising thoughts, tasks, and actions, taking up brain power and space to try to keep you organised. You are constantly receiving information and your brain is distorting, generalising, and deleting information, subconsciously creating priorities to create ease.

You may even notice yourself taking a sigh of relief when decluttering, which in turn, creates greater space in your body. We can then look within and move through your four pillars as you declutter your mind, heart, body, and spirit.

I would also highly recommend decluttering things, people, situations, and spaces that you feel may drain you or have a negative effect on you. This includes mainstream media, social media, and unhealthy social or work groups. Some situations or spaces may seem unavoidable, such as work or going out in the community, grocery shopping, etc. However, remember you choose who you wish to connect and spend time with, what you view, your social groups and social media, and where you focus your energy.

Maybe there is a better time to go out shopping when there are fewer people or perhaps a higher-habit you can implement in place of your morning social media scrolling. This is all part of your journey, developing self-mastery over your human experience and having the power of choice on where you focus your time, energy, and effort.

Energy And Social Media Detox

Our energy can be drained in a number of ways: social media, TV, news, friends, social circles, movies, music, food, alcohol, and drugs, to name a few. These things can distract us away from what is truly important or healthy, greatly impacting our human experience.

We live in a society where much of what we do all day can be spent looking at a screen. We have all become a little addicted to the dopamine hit we receive when the phone pings: a message, notification, email, or social media alerts. Every time we receive a notification, it subconsciously sets off a response in our neurochemistry, positively or negatively.

Often, people are constantly checking their devices in fear of missing out. What we are viewing on social media, or the news in general, can be misleading or not a true reflection or representation of 'real life'. This leads to living in a constant high-stress state, leaking your power, which reduces self-confidence and leads to higher levels of anxiety and stress.

Doing an energy and social media detox will help to restore your energy, clear your mind, give you more time to do things that add benefit to your life, and bring more peace and calm to your life. Think of it like a junk food detox. We all know that junk food is not good for us if we consume it in high volumes regularly. However, an occasional treat is OK.

Reflect on how often you reach for your phone first thing upon waking? When was the last time you checked your phone for notifications? How much time have you wasted on endless and aimless scrolling? In order to receive the benefits of an energy and social media detox, you don't have to go cold turkey, but minimising your exposure to social media and energy 'vampires' or leaks will begin to restore your energy immediately.

If you choose to continue viewing mainstream media, news, certain movies, and social media, ensure that you allow time to yourself to clear your energy and recharge afterwards. We are consciously creating our life and choosing our human experience, so be sure to clear away what you don't want and focus on what you do.

An energy and social media detox is a great way to reclaim your power, connect, and realign with your infinite spiritual being.

I have included some guidelines for an energy and social media detox in the *SacredPlay*. This will help you to monitor the effects these things have on your energy. Give it a try at least once – you won't know that you need it until you try it. You may be surprised at the results.

As you move throughout your environment and decluttering, ask if the item brings you joy. If it is something that you are ready to relinquish, ask if it may bring another joy. That way you are giving with a grateful heart.

When self-reflecting and moving through your internal pillars of mind, heart, body, and spirit, to clear all that no longer serves you, ask yourself these questions:

What thoughts, ideas, and patterns am I holding onto that no longer serve me? Is this thought useful?

What are you holding onto in your heart-space? Are you still holding onto past heartbreaks, caging your heart from opening and experiencing love on all levels?

What are you still carrying in your Body Temple? Look at where you may be experiencing pain, dis-ease, or discomfort in your body. This is your body's way of communicating with you that you are holding onto past hurt and trauma. What can you clear from your body to experience miracles of healing?

How To Do An Energy And Social Media Detox

First, decide on how many days you'd like to do the detox. Then gather some stones and crystals to you, the same number for the length of days that you wish to do the detox. For example, if you are doing the detox for 10 days, gather 10 crystals or stones. This will help you to keep track of your days and your energy.

Do an assessment on how you are presently feeling. Use the space below to record how you feel when you are on social media, watching movies or TV, or are spending time around certain friends. Then as you are navigating through your detox, I encourage you to journal how you are feeling each day.

Remember, we need to replace habits with higher-habits. Simply cutting these things from your life can be detrimental. Going cold turkey does not work for everyone because it sends a signal to the brain triggering a fear response. Monitoring your progress and replacing these habits with higher-habits that serve you will help lead you towards success, giving you a calmer, more harmonious humanly experience.

At first, you may not be aware of how you feel; however, during the course of your detox, you will begin to notice changes, feel lighter, have more energy and enjoy a greater sense of peace.

We will also need to establish what higher-habits you can replace existing habits with. I have provided a list below you may wish to use.

Here is a list of higher-habits you may wish to incorporate into your life. Where you may previously have reached for your phone to check social media, watched the news, played video games, consumed drugs or alcohol, choose some activities from the list below that resonate with you.

- Meditation.
- Listen to high-vibrational music.
- Dance.
- Call a friend.
- Spend time in nature.
- Do puzzles, word searches, sudoku.
- Read a book.
- Exercise, go for a walk, go to the gym, or do some yoga.
- Play a board game or cards.
- Journal or write.
- Learn a new skill, language, or hobby.
- Paint, draw, sketch, cross-stitch, knit, crochet; get creative with your hands.
- Take an online course.
- Create a vision or intention board.
- Declutter your home, car, purse, bag, and work space.
- Listen to podcasts or audio books.
- Plus, so much more…Get creative and explore new ways to effectively use your time and energy. They don't need to cost money. There is an abundance of free activities and resources to be creative with.

You will need support on your journey. Tell people that you are taking an energy and social media detox and that they will need to contact you directly if they wish to connect with you. Delete the apps from your phone or device. This is the only way to guarantee that you will not be tempted to 'just check in'.

If you are feeling FOMO (the fear of missing out), then connect with your family and friends through more meaningful ways. If you follow inspirational people on social media, then turn on their podcasts and YouTube videos. Get on to emails and communicate with long distance friends. Pick up the phone and actually call people: family and loved ones.

You will find yourself developing more meaningful connections and feeling more fulfilled in life. This is all in support of raising your vibe and embodying your sovereignty and Higher-Self.

Ask yourself this question for each of the categories below:

- **How do I feel when I watch TV, movies, social media, listen to certain music, hang out with some of my friends, eat certain foods, consume drugs or alcohol, play video games, attend social gatherings, or connect in online groups? Remember not to judge yourself, simply witness what comes up and record it below.**

Category	How do I feel when I consume these energies? (For example, "Whenever I am watching the news, I feel angry and fearful." "When I am on social media, I feel unworthy and not enough."
Social media	
Movies	
Food	
Alcohol	
Drugs	
Gaming	
TV	
News	

Music	
Social Situations	
Friends	
Other: (add any others here or use your journal to record more)	

Now you are better equipped to complete your energy and social media detox.

Use the crystals, pebbles, or stones that you have collected (one for each day of your detox, ie 10 crystals for 10 days).

At the beginning of each day, take one stone or crystal from one bowl or bag and place it into another. I would recommend labelling the bowls day 1 and day 10 or 'beginning' and 'completion' so that you know from which one you are taking to which you are placing.

Meditate for a few moments, then reflect on how you are feeling. How are you emotionally? Do you feel like you are missing out? Are you feeling anxiety about missing out, or are you feeling more at peace and have more time? Journal your feelings and findings in the spaces below.

When you have completed your detox process, place all the stones or crystals back in the original cloth pouch and leave them on your altar or in a private place until you wish to use them again. You may also wish to return them to Mother Earth if you gathered them from nature. Thank her for the blessing of using these as tools in your detox when you return them.

Day	Reflections
Day 1	
Day 2	
Day 3	
Day 4	

Day 5	
Day 6	
Day 7	
Day 8	
Day 9	
Day 10	
Add extra days if you wish.	

"Shadow work is the path of the heart warrior."

CARL JUNG

14
Spiritual By-Passing

What Is Spiritual By-Passing?

Not everything in life is 'love and light' as many spiritual communities preach or have us believe. Spiritual by-passing is a way many hide behind spiritual practices to avoid or acknowledge their feelings. This is often used to repress emotions such as anger, and it is designed to protect the ego and hide insecurities.

This can also distance one from others, believing themselves to be superior, more 'spiritual', and cause separation.

The term 'spiritual by-passing' was first coined by Professor John Welwood, where in his practice he would notice others, as well as himself, using spiritual ideas and practices as a way to side-step or avoid facing unresolved issues, psychological wounds, and unfinished developmental tasks. Rather than facing the tough questions and emotional wounds, people would dismiss them using spiritual explanations.

Spiritual by-passing doesn't resolve the issue, it merely glosses over it and, ultimately, can stifle your growth and development in your Earthly experience.

Some examples of spiritual by-passing include:

- Avoiding feelings of anger.
- Believing in your own spiritual superiority.
- Hiding from insecurities, often subconsciously.
- Professing that traumatic events must serve as "learning experiences" or that there is a silver lining behind every negative experience.
- Believing that spiritual practices such as meditation or prayer are always positive, even using these practices as a means to 'escape' life.
- Extremely high, often unattainable, idealism.
- Feelings of detachment.
- Focusing only on spirituality and ignoring the present.
- Only focusing on the positive or being overly optimistic.
- Projecting your own negative feelings onto others.
- Pretending that things are fine when they are clearly not.
- Thinking that people can overcome their problems through positive thinking.
- Thinking that you must "rise above" your emotions.
- Denying and repressing emotions.

Whilst this may leave us feeling good in the short-term, it does not resolve the underlying issue, and in fact, leaves the problem to linger on long-term. It is often a way of dismissing a difficult situation because we don't want to face the problem, hence 'making us feel better'.

Spiritual by-passing can also have a negative effect on our Earthly experience. It can leave us feeling anxious, causes separation from others due to believing we are superior, masking difficult emotions, not expressing feelings, repressing 'negative' emotions such as anger, jealously, disgust, shame, or annoyance. It can lead to attachment and control problems, confusion, and feelings of shame.

How To Navigate Spiritual By-Passing

Spiritual by-passing neglects an important truth; that we are spiritual beings having a human experience and part of this experience is feeling all of our emotions and navigating life's highs and lows. Life is not all love and light. The contrast gives us clarity. When we experience lows, we grow and expand; when we experience highs, we are in alignment and following our dharma and spiritual being. Both are required and necessary.

Some things we can do to avoid spiritual by-passing is simply feeling your emotions and avoid labelling them as 'good' or 'bad'. Our emotional experiences are a part of life, and they serve a purpose. Witness them, but don't attach to them. Rather than avoiding negative emotions, use them to propel you towards positive action.

Wearing rose-coloured glasses and ignoring an issue isn't going to make it better or go away. Feeling an uncomfortable emotion is often telling us we are out of alignment and something needs to change. Look for the transformational value of what the uncomfortable emotion is spurring you towards. I call this shadow-values, finding the value in our shadow.

Sacred Play

Reflect on your life and see where you might be spiritually by-passing. What emotions are you avoiding because they may be uncomfortable or not considered 'spiritual', such as anger or jealousy?

Grab your trusty journal or write your findings in the space provided below. Remember not to judge what comes up. We don't want to label emotions as 'good' or 'bad'; we simply want to witness them and see what they are attempting to teach us.

Where have I been spiritually by-passing? Am I feeling anger, jealously, shame, etc? Do I allow myself to feel these emotions when they arise?

What are these experiences trying to teach me? Am I holding onto insecurities or attachment?

"To err is human, to forgive is divine."

ALEXANDER POPE

15
The Transformative Power Of Forgiveness

The Power Of Forgiveness

Forgiveness is a deep spiritual practice and takes daily focus and attention. Part of our self-mastery and living in harmony with our spiritual being requires us to forgive.

We must also forgive ourselves, as much as we do others.

By no means are we condoning what has been said or done. Forgiveness does, however, release us from blame, guilt, and shame. These qualities have no transformational value. When we hold hate in our heart or we are unable to forgive another being, we are holding ourselves into bondage.

Not forgiving someone is said to be like carrying that person around on your back through life. Consciously or unconsciously, they continue to impact your life and your choices. Remember, you are worthy of living a blissful and abundant life.

For every 'superhero' there must be a 'villain', otherwise heroes are redundant. No one would need saving and we would all be living an empowered and enriched life. In truth, we all have the power within to 'save ourselves', be our own hero or heroine of our story. Our decisions are our greatest superpower, and in any moment in time, we can choose to shift something that is no longer serving us, simply by choosing to change.

I invite you to move away from the notion of 'good' and 'bad" or 'good versus evil'. We are all experiencing life and doing the best we can from our level of consciousness at the time. Often, we are acting upon or making a decision based on our experiences throughout life or what we think is expected of us. We have all come to this Earth with a sacred soul contract, inviting certain experiences and lessons to learn, grow, enrich, and embody as we move towards enlightenment.

When we accept that everyone is doing the very best they can according to their level of consciousness, it releases us from judgement and the emotional entrapment that can envelop you. However, it is important to establish boundaries so this behaviour does not continue to impact your life moving forward.

There are many stages to forgiveness. Often people say, "I forgive you -- because I know karma will get you eventually," or that, "The Universe will take care of it." This is not true forgiveness because the desire for retaliation, either from the Universe or through karma, is still alive within you. You may have 'put down the gun' so to speak, however, you have not surrendered the desire to shoot, still expecting 'justice to be done'.

What Is True Forgiveness?

The stages of forgiveness are as follows:

- A willingness to forgive.
- Practising forgiveness.
- Being willing to see things from the other's perspective.
- Wishing them well.
- Doing something symbolic towards them; sending positive energy towards them.

All forgiveness is self-forgiveness. By forgiving others it frees us from victimhood and gives us a sense of peace. I often get asked, "How long does this process take?" Only you will know when you have truly forgiven someone. This could take hours, days, weeks, or even years. Don't focus on the time as there are many levels to forgiveness.

You will know true forgiveness when your thoughts about this person or situation no longer stir up emotions within you and you feel neutral – this is how you will know that you have truly forgiven another or yourself.

Below is a beautiful forgiveness protocol that you can follow. It immediately releases transgressions you may feel within you, and the relief you feel afterwards is very cathartic. Only if, however, you truly choose to release and forgive. You always have the power of choice. Are you ready to forgive? This is an imperative question to ask yourself, and only you can answer. I invite you to do so truthfully, and as a result, you will feel the power of that decision.

When choosing to complete the forgiveness protocol, you may require to perform it several times, until you no longer feel 'emotion or energy' towards the person you are forgiving. Remember, this may also be yourself. Forgiveness for yourself is part of our humanly experience and paramount to living a truly abundant, blissful life.

Forgiveness Protocol

Do this as often as you feel the need.

> Sit and meditate for a few minutes and ground your energy.
>
> Visualise the person you wish to forgive. Imagine them as if they are in front of you.
>
> Say, the name of the person. Call them in 3 times. You may wish to use a photo or write their name on a piece of paper. Repeat the following:
>
> *"(Name), I now forgive you, for everything that you have ever done to me, consciously or unconsciously, in this lifetime or any other. I forgive you; I forgive you; I forgive you."*
>
> Breathe in and release. Repeat this 3 times.
>
> Now ask them to forgive you. (This is vitally important. You need to take responsibility for your part to enact true forgiveness).

> *"(Name), I now ask that you forgive me, for everything that I have ever done that has hurt you, consciously or unconsciously, in this lifetime or any other. Please forgive me, please forgive me, please forgive me".*
>
> Breathe in and release. Repeat this step 3 times.
>
> Imagine, visualise, or feel the lines or cords of energy joining you to the other person. Raise your hand and bring it down, like you are cutting the lines and cords, and say:
>
> *"I now clear all karmic ties between us, across all time, space, dimension, and reality. I set myself free and reclaim my spirit now. May you be free and may all good things happen to you. Thank you, Thank you, Thank you".*
>
> Breathe in and release. Repeat this step 3 times.

Forgiveness will empower and heal you. Forgiveness is love: unconditional love to yourself and another. You are a hu-man being, 'God-like' love in present state, here and now. Choosing to forgive will make you feel more balanced, strong, powerful, and more enlightened, reinstating your 'God-source' energy into your human experience. That lights me up. Reclaiming your God-self is a powerful state of be-ing. May you always remember this state, choose to live from here, and feel the unconditional love and compassion flow through you unto others.

Often, the person you need to forgive the most is yourself. Forgiving yourself is no different to forgiving the other person. You simply go through the same process and follow the steps.

Visualise yourself as you would visualise any other person or look in the mirror as you follow the above forgiveness protocol.

Sacred Play

Practice forgiveness for approximately 15 minutes per day. Longer if desired or required.

Spend time daily in quiet meditation and undertake the Forgiveness Protocol.

Reciting positive affirmations for forgiveness will also help release attachments and judgements and help you to forgive.

Some examples of positive affirmations for forgiveness are:

- I take full responsibility for my actions and I forgive myself for all that I have done, knowingly or unknowingly, to hurt myself or others.
- I release myself from the bondage of un-forgiveness and forgive myself and others.
- Wonderful, wonderful me, I now set myself free.

Undergo the forgiveness protocol to help you forgive yourself and others as many times as you feel necessary. Remember there is no time limit or constraints on how long this is going to take. Everyone is different; our experiences and life path shape us all in different ways. You are an infinite spiritual being having a human experience, and I wish to remind you of your unique individuality, sovereignty, and power.

Conduct the forgiveness protocol and journal how this feels for you. Witnessing your feelings and emotions will help you to determine how you are releasing and forgiving others and yourself.

How do I feel after doing the Forgiveness Protocol?

Construct some of your own forgiveness mantras and positive affirmations and write them below or in your journal. You may also like to write them on sticky-notes and place them around your home as a reminder to practice forgiveness because you are worthy.

My forgiveness mantras and positive affirmations are:

"The dark night of the soul is a journey into the light, a journey from your darkness into the strength and hidden resources of your soul."

CAROLINE MYSS

16
Dark Night Of The Soul

What Is Dark Night Of The Soul?

The term 'dark night of the soul' originated in the 16th century by the Spanish poet St John of the Cross who wrote an unnamed poem, comprising two book-length commentaries which describes a spiritual crisis on the journey to union with God. This poem later became entitled Dark Night of the Soul.

It spells out the agony that we as humans often place upon ourselves, remembering our Divinity, our god-like nature, and return to union with God and our Highest-Level self.

Dark night of the soul is also often referred to as an 'ego death'. It is not the soul that is dying, rather a part of the 'ego': the death of a reality or belief you previously held regarding something in your life. It can be triggered by an external circumstance, such as the passing of a loved one. A part of your reality has collapsed, leaving you feeling like you have been left in the dark. As a result, many experience their spiritual awakening in this way. You emerge, awakening, into something deeper, a greater level of consciousness, a deeper sense of purpose, and a greater feeling of connectedness.

Whilst death can be painful, this is not death in the literal sense; however, an egoistic part of you dies: the death of the old self and the birth of the true self. Things that you previously gave meaning to, either from conditioning, domestication, society, upbringing, etc, dissolve away. This is a return to your true state of being, an infinite spiritual being, having a human experience.

Ego Death

The ego keeps us stuck and small, whilst the soul desires expansion and growth. The soul often initiates an ego death and it can feel like you are experiencing an existential crisis. What you perhaps previously thought was meaningful has become meaningless. We experience a shift in perspective.

Things you previously may have attached your identity to or things that lead from your ego, such as career, money, car, relationships – you suddenly realise these things don't actually make you happy and have little to no meaning. Therefore, we lose our desire in pursuing or acquiring them because we now recognise they are only based on ego. We no longer know who we are or what we want. This is the transition of dark night of the soul.

It is when we resist change, attempt to control and retain attachments, that we experience the pain, confusion, and the dark night. During this time, your soul is actually pulling you back towards love, joy, expansion, and freedom. It is returning you to your true state of being. Your soul is always connected to Infinite Source Energy, which is a state of Love and knows what is best for you.

Rebirth

> *"Sometimes when you're in a dark place you think you've been buried, but you've actually been planted."*
> *- Christine Caine*

This is your spiritual awakening. When we allow ourselves to be guided by our soul, Higher-Self, and Infinite Source Energy, we feel more connected: life takes on new meaning. We feel we have a new identity and a new purpose in life.

Dark night of the soul can be associated with the caterpillar and butterfly analogy. The caterpillar must remain in the darkness of the cocoon, undergoing its transformation, to emerge as the butterfly. It accepted its fate and what feels like a literal death to emerge into the next level of transformation and true state of being: the butterfly.

Navigating Through Soul's Dark Night

When we are experiencing dark night of the soul, remember to be compassionate with yourself. You are not your thoughts. Don't attach yourself to words or emotions; witness them and see what comes through for you. The 'ego death' is not something to be 'fixed'. It is a part of your human expansion. Resistance is futile and will only cause further pain and discomfort. The invitation is to surrender and go with the flow.

Follow the guidance of your Higher-Self. What does it want to teach you? What is it trying to show you?

The more you hold onto the past, the more you suffer. Your soul is guiding you to a greater level of awareness, consciousness, and enlightenment. Your journey will be much smoother and transition more quickly if you allow yourself to flow.

This can be an emotional ride. Allow your emotions to surface, and again, remember to simply witness, without judgement and not attach to them. The ego will resist; it doesn't like change and wants to avoid pain. However, allow your soul to be your guide. Be patient and trust the process.

There is no set timeframe and everyone's journey is unique. When you see the light emerging, show yourself compassion: you have been altered. Like the caterpillar becoming the butterfly, it needs to adjust to its new stage of being. It may result in changes in careers, relationships, friendships, or moving home. Do what you feel your soul is calling you to do. We seek answers by asking the right questions. This is a soul activation; we need to release the ego and embrace your true infinite nature and being.

Reflect back on your life and think about when you may have experienced a dark night of the soul. Ask yourself the following questions and write you answers below or in your beloved journal.

What time in my life did I experience a dark night of the soul?

What changes emerged through me during my dark night of the soul?

What opportunities did I become open to after my dark night of the soul?

What changes can I make in my life to be more in alignment with my soul?

"When the heart weeps for what it has lost, the soul rejoices for what it has found."

ANCIENT SUFI PROVERB

17
The Gift Of Grief

What Is Grief?

Throughout our life, we all share two inevitable events: birth and death. Whilst we often eagerly anticipate and await the arrival of a birth, we seem to shun death, attempt to ignore it, or shift our focus onto other things when death approaches.

We often don't get to prepare for death in the same manner we may do for a birth. Death can oftentimes be sudden, and then we feel a loss.

This chapter speaks to my heart and affected the most self-reflection. All the teaching and lessons in this handbook I have personally applied and taught to many, which is all testimony to their value and effectiveness in affecting change. So to with this chapter.

I am a firm believer in teaching and sharing what one personally does. I walk my talk, which is why this chapter was a late addition. My mother passed-over a few months earlier when writing this, unexpectedly. This called upon me to reflect deeply on my beliefs; all my knowledge and wisdom came into effect, necessitating me to check-in on my heart, mind, body, and spirit.

All my teachings came into play. I had resources to call upon to help me navigate my 'loss' and find the gift in my grief. I understood soul contracts, our Earthly human experience, and our soul group connection. Now was time to integrate these lessons into my heart, mind, body, and spirit from a grief perspective. I called upon my Highest-Level Self to help me navigate this new experience, to bring calm from my soul to my physical being without by-passing this beautiful gift.

Whilst my father passed-over 5 years earlier, the grief was different. My father and I had a fractured relationship in the Earthly realm that required a consolidation of understanding our soul contracts to navigate the grief.

The passing of my mother, who was very near and dear to me, came as a shock. She had dementia and I had been caring for her for the 8 years prior before she passed. It is often said when caring for a loved one who is nearing the end of their Earthly experience, one grieves anticipating their death. During my research, I discovered this to be termed anticipatory grief.

One might think that makes things easier when the loved one passes; however, it does not – certainly not in my experience navigating my own grief, nor from all the people I have taught and researched when writing this chapter.

The passing of my beloved Baron was another beautiful experience of a beloved being transitioning over. Baron was my Poodle X Shi Tzu dog who I raised from an 8 week old puppy until he transitioned over the rainbow bridge when he was 16.5 years old. He was always by my side and as he matured, required greater care. The love of a beloved pet is very sacred and is a beautiful addition to our human experience. Each held a gift.

My *SacredPlay* came to the fore. Attention on my heart-temple, mind-temple, body-temple, and Spirit was paramount for me to feel. I put into action every step, tool, sacred connection, and any innate resources I held which then became part of the *SacredPlay* you will see outlined below. It has been a blessing. As with all journeys, each person's experience is unique; however, I wish to relay that this 'work' is always worth doing and is profoundly impactful in living a harmonious, joyful experience.

Remember, we are not here to shame, numb, or avoid our emotions, especially grief. Our desire is to witness them, but not attach ourselves to them and so we can uncover what they are here to teach us. We are here to feel, play, and experience life, all aspects of it.

Grief is the pain that comes from loss, which includes many emotions and expresses itself mentally, emotionally, behaviourally, and through physical pain.

There are many different types of grief, such as the passing of a loved one, diagnosis of a serious illness, the end of a job, a relationship, a divorce, or when a beloved pet dies. I have also had many of these experiences in this lifetime and may even have many more – as no doubt you may have or will experience.

We feel grief when we feel loss; a piece of us has been removed somehow, loss, longing, or feeling lost are some of the emotions that are felt. Understanding grief, the sense of loss, the emerging emotions, and physical response will help us navigate this beautiful human experience.

The Different Types Of Grief

Below is a list of the different types of grief:

- **Acute grief.** This sudden onset of grief occurs in the initial period after a loss.
- **Anticipatory grief.** This occurs when we know a loved one is expecting to die, either due to age, illness, following an accident, etc. This can also occur when a job contract or a close relationship is coming to an end.
- **Integrated grief.** This is the result of adapting to our loss. Grief finds a place in our life.
- **Complicated grief.** This occurs over a long period of time when a person feels deep emotional pain and somehow hopes or expects their loved one might reappear. They don't see a way forward. This type of grief dominates their thoughts and feelings and their life.
- **Delayed grief.** This type of grief happens initially when a person stays strong for others or their own survival. This can occur after a job loss, divorce, or following the death of a loved one.
- **Disenfranchised grief.** Also known as invisible grief, this is experienced when it is not recognised or openly acknowledged by society. This can include loss of a parent or partner, going through divorce, loss of an unborn child,

infertility, miscarriage, or abortion. This may also occur after surviving a sexual assault and feeling the loss of trust, self-identity, self-esteem, and a prior world view.

- **Distorted grief.** This occurs when a person experiences intense or extreme emotions that manifests into self-destructive behaviour or hostility.
- **Exaggerated grief.** This occurs when a person is grieving over an extended period of time and results in mental health disorders, nightmares, suicidal thoughts, phobias, and self-destructive behaviours.
- **Masked grief.** This is a result of when a person hides their grief from the outside world and grieves in silence.
- **Inhibited grief.** This occurs when a person exhibits a few signs of grief, but mostly grieves internally or out of sight. This can manifest in the body as headaches, nausea, or general aches and pains.
- **Shortened grief.** This is when a person quickly navigates through their grief after a loss. This may occur after a divorce, job loss, or death of a loved one.
- **Collective grief.** This is experienced when a tribe, community, society, town, country, or world is collectively feeling a sadness or loss, such as a global pandemic, war, natural disasters, or the death of an significant figure.

It is important to identify the type of grief you are experiencing to help navigate you through your journey. Some processes to help you navigate through grief are in the *SacredPlay*. However, you may also like to seek out support from a health professional or spiritual mentor who is trained in grief to guide you.

When Grief Knocks

When we have experienced a loss, grief comes knocking at our door. It sneaks up on us and can occur at any time and often in the most inconvenient places.

I remember ordering a coffee at my local café, and as the waiter delivered it with his usual joy and effervescent energy, I broke down and became 'overwhelmed' with grief. You see, grief can sneak up on you at any moment, at any time, reminding us of a loss we are feeling.

Overwhelm is another emotion that I like to shift to 'overflow'. This gives us permission to allow the energy to flow, witnessing it and not attaching to it, without judgement, shame, or guilt.

Healing grief is by no means linear as it was once thought. We will shift through various emotions throughout the process in its own unique timeline. There is no specified timeframe to 'move on' from grief. In fact, we learn to find joy and bliss even whilst living with our perceived loss.

Each person's grief is as unique as their fingerprint and is expressed in different ways. It is an opportunity to expand and grow our conscious awareness as part of our Earthly experience.

It is important to know that healing is not only possible, it is imperative. You are an infinite being from pure Source energy, a Divine incarnation of the Cosmos, and we are not placed on this Earth to suffer only loss and pain. We have chosen to come to this Earth to experience life, its vastness, richness, and pleasures.

Navigating Through Grief

Loss and grief provides an opportunity for deep inner reflection and ultimately, transformation. After our loss, we often ask questions such as, "Why did this happen to me?" or "What will I do now?" or "How am I supposed to live without them?" Although these questions come from our human self, stemming from our grief and loss, when asked from a spiritual context, they provide the power of transformation.

As a spiritual being, we know and understand that we all come from Love and have come to this Earth with a soul contract.

I encourage you to explore these questions regarding your pain and loss from a spiritual perspective. It is absolutely possible to live happily and thrive after we experience loss. As a spiritual being, not only is it possible, it is required of us to continue to expand and grow as part of our Earthly human experience. We can still find joy whilst experiencing grief. The two are not mutually exclusive, and they help us to navigate towards unconditional love and bliss.

For many of us throughout our life, we have been conditioned to believe that we experience our relationships and love through our physical senses, to whom we can see, feel, hear, and touch. Again, this is limited to our Earthly experience, forgetting that we are spiritual beings and that 'nothing or no-one' truly 'dies'; we return to oneness, God, and Universal Source Energy where we are eternal cosmic beings.

Remembering this, we rethink how we love, how we relate, and how we live in this Earthly realm, and in doing so, undergo spiritual self-discovery. We begin reclaiming an unconditional loving relationship from within and extend that love to others. Instead of merely 'surviving' our grief or attempting to cope, we transcend these experiences to live an authentic joyful and blissful human experience through a spiritual transformation.

We want to navigate our grief by taking back our heart, mind, and life – from coping with our loss to freely and unconditionally living and loving our life.

Through our spiritual practice, rituals, and self-inquiry, we develop a deeper awareness of Universal Love, gain greater insight and wisdom, and ultimately have the ability to alchemise our grief to joy and happiness.

There are a number of different self-healing modalities you can implement to help you navigate through loss and grief of any kind. Intention, affirmations, practice, rituals, and self-reflective questions are a few ways to help navigate you through to living and loving with joy and bliss. All healing is self-healing; it must come from within.

With daily practice and rituals, this allows time and space for your grief to be witnessed and transmuted with gentle loving and compassionate energy. By doing this, you are giving yourself the gift of healing. I have included some in the *SacredPlay* for you to undertake.

Living with self-mastery, practising non-attachment, and living with unconditional love are all ways to remember the infinite expansive being that you are, where there is no 'death' or 'loss'.

We are always connected with all living beings, whether they are transitioned or living.

Sacred Play

Navigating through loss and grief to thriving and loving requires self-reflection, self-awareness, self-compassion, and unconditional self-love.

Below are some ways to help navigate through grief. Even if you have not experienced the loss of a loved one, you may have experienced grief in other ways. Engage these practices below to help navigate through grief and live with bliss and joy.

Gratitude

It's often challenging to feel sadness and loss when we are expressing deep gratitude. Take some deep breaths and write down 3 things you are grateful for. In fact, why stop there? Keep going and write as many things as you can in the time you have.

Affirmations

Affirmations are a beautiful and powerful way of reclaiming your mind and heart. Write your own empowering affirmation below or in your trusty journal. You may also like to write this on your mirror or on sticky-notes and place them where they catch your eye. These will help activate a positive response in your subconscious whenever you see them.

Intentions

Living with intention and setting an intention for you day, practice and ritual will amplify the energy and healing of your grief.

Self-Care

Self-care is another form of self-love and an important part of your healing journey. Make time for self-care daily. You may wish to give yourself time to meditate, complete rituals, have a massage, a bath, take a walk in nature or on the beach, take time out to read a book. We are allowing time for ourselves and our healing journey.

Self-Inquiry And Self-Reflective Questions

Allowing time for deep introspection by asking questions will uncover the source of our loss and grief and enable us to transmute it. You may choose to journal these questions daily or do one each day and cycle through them. Daily journalling gives you space to pour your thoughts and heart out without judgement. It also allows new insights to flow through. Do this as part of your *SacredPlay*.

- How can I move forward?
- What good is here that I presently cannot see?
- What do I need to know today?
- What is my purpose today?
- What is my intention today?
- What or who inspires me today?
- What brought me joy yesterday?
- What are 3 things I am grateful for today?

Rituals

Rituals are a beautiful way to give space to your emotions and healing. Outlined below are simple steps to undertake when performing your ritual.

- **Presence.** Set aside a time and place to perform your ritual without distraction, being able to give your entire presence.
- **Intention.** Set an intention for your ritual. Ask yourself these questions: "What is it I would like to happen?" and "What do I need in this moment?" Keeping your intention clear in your mind will amplify your ritual and healing energy.
- **Symbolism.** Symbols place an important part in bringing meaning to your ritual. These can be flowers, candles, crystals, photographs, jewellery, incense, or anything else you feel will support you on your journey.
- **Keep an open heart.** You may experience a range of emotions during your ritual. Keep an open heart and allow what flows through without judgement. Show deep love and compassion for yourself.
- **Spirit.** Remembering we are spiritual beings connected to Infinite Source Energy, we also want to acknowledge this during our ritual. You may use whatever means you wish to acknowledge the Universe.

Here are 6 easy steps for you to follow to create a ritual, though I also encourage you to create your own. It's important to remember you don't need fancy or 'special items' for you to complete your ritual. Use things you already have around your home along with the power of your presence and intention.

1. Gather your sacred items and any symbolism you wish to incorporate into your ritual. A candle, pen and note paper, or journal is essential. The Universe loves detail and handwritten notes are a powerful way to align your heart with Spirit. You may also like to gather crystals, essential oils and fresh flowers, a smudge stick, sage, or other 'clearing' tools.

2. Create a sacred space. Clear your space before the ritual using your smudge stick or other clearing tools and remove any distractions. Create an altar or centrepiece, light a candle, put on some meditation music, and really get into the vibe. Make your space beautiful to allow flow.

3. Set your intention and meditate. Sit still for at least 5 minutes and focus on your breath. Call in your guides, angels – whatever your connection with Source is – and ask to be guided soulfully and for your highest good.

4. Write down anything that flows through. Keep your heart open and allow it to flow from your heart to paper.

5. Surrender. Trust that the Universe knows your intentions and knows what is best for you. The Universe sees the grand plan for your life. We want to surrender to Source and allow healing and miracles to flow into your life. Be open and ready to receive.

6. Sit and visualise what a life filled with bliss and happiness looks and feels like. Allow yourself to see it as if you are living it in this very moment. Bring it into the now. See it, feel it, breathe it in! Say "It is done. It is done. It is done," to seal it in.

7. Close your circle. Whenever you are ready, thank the Universe, Spirit, and any guides you called upon for joining you in your ritual. Blow out the candle to signify when you are done.

"The secret of your success is found in your daily routine."

JOHN MAXWELL

18
Daily Rituals, Application, And Integration

Daily Habits

It is important to integrate your learnings into daily practices and rituals to create higher-habits so you can thoroughly thrive through your human experience and live a more fulfilled, purposeful life.

If the "secret to your success is found in your daily routine", then I invite you to create a daily routine that will lead you to be your secret to your success.

Firstly, it is important to decide what 'success' looks and feels like. What 'success' may be to you will look and feel very different for another. This is another opportunity to go within. Look to your hierarchy of values, they will point you towards your success. Your true definition of success comes from within and not chasing the 'latest or greatest' or 'keeping up with the Joneses'.

Once you have established what your success looks and feels like (I have a *SacredPlay* for you to do to help you), below are 5 key steps to help you create a routine and embody your daily practice to amplify your success:

- **Your 'upon-rising routine'.** How you start each day will greatly impact how your day will flow. Establish an effective daily routine that serves you. Here are some of the rituals we explored throughout the book.
  - Start each day with an **intention**.
  - Develop an attitude of **gratitude**. Take a few moments each day to express your heartfelt gratitude.
  - Be willing to **surrender** to the Infinite, Cosmos, Universe, God.
  - Recite daily **affirmations, mantras,** and **declarations**.
  - **Journal** daily. Your intentions, goals, and manifestations: all that is wishing to emerge and flow through you.
  - **Reflect** daily. Take time for self-reflection to integrate lessons learned.
  - Practice **forgiveness** daily.
  - Establish **higher-habits**.
  - Expect **miracles** to show up in your life.
- **Meditate** daily. For at least 20 minutes sit and deeply listen to what is wanting to be expressed. Take time to visualise your values and goals, your path and purpose. There is an old yogi saying that "one must meditate for 20 minutes per day, unless you are busy, then you should meditate longer." Use this as a benchmark.
- **Schedule.** What gets scheduled, gets done. Block time out for yourself, your values, work, play, family, self-care, etc, each day. This will become your blueprint for your week. Write it down and schedule it in your calendar.

- **Reflect.** Take time each day to self-reflect on how you are impacting the world. This is not a time to beat yourself up on what you did or did not do. It is a time to reflect on the lessons learned and realign your behaviour towards your values, path, and purpose.
- **Follow your dharma.** Work towards your goals and dreams, your passion and purpose. Schedule time each day that moves you closer towards your dharma.
- **Read and learn.** Educate yourself on something that lights you up, that feels in alignment with your infinite spiritual being. Read, learn, grow. Be a perpetual student.

These simple little rituals only take a few minutes each day and may be compressed on days where you may be time-poor; however, I invite you to allow time for yourself each day. Fill your cup first so that you are full and can be more of service to your community, relationships, and others.

Remember to read, study, and listen to further your knowledge. Do something daily that moves you towards your Higher-Self and establishes a stronger connection with the Universe towards your path and purpose. Listen to podcasts from mentors and teachers who are doing the work you desire to do. Watch instructional videos, do an online course or further study, read a book on productivity or an area of key interest. Think like a student: be open to learning. Every master thinks like a beginner.

Allowing time for integration allows your higher-habits to be embodied and enables you to develop self-mastery. They become second nature and you will express a new way of being, one that is aligned and purposeful. This is how we programme our subconscious mind so that it serves us abundantly, not from a state of fear or lack.

Act on these today and live the life of your dreams. Develop and commit to a daily ritual that you follow each day, either in your online calendar or purchase a beautiful diary or calendar that you can carry around with you: make notes, journal findings, inspiration, and take inspired action from them.

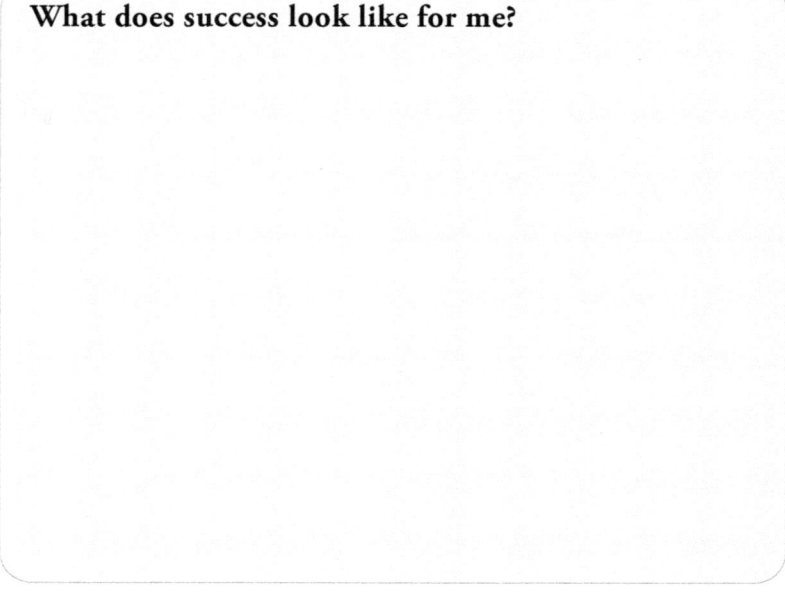

What does success look like for me?

What does success feel like for me?

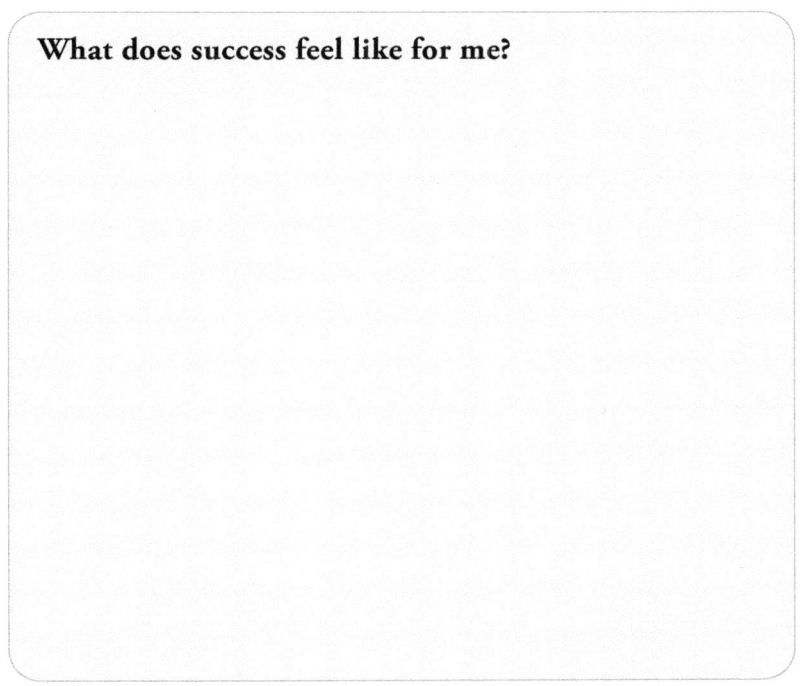

Create a daily ritual to enable you to develop higher-habits.

Even if you are a shift-worker, you can still develop a daily ritual. Your 'rising-routine' will simply shift to when you wake up. Upon rising is the best time for you to take time for yourself – this is before you pick up your phone, connect with your partner, manage the kids and household, etc. This is an essential time in your routine to focus on what you are wanting to create and how your day will flow. The other great time to connect with yourself is just before bed.

Take 10 minutes to yourself and vision your life as you desire it to be.

"The journey of a thousand miles begins with a single step."

LAO TZU

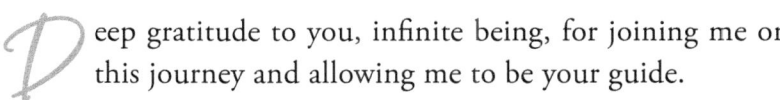

It's Only The Beginning

Deep gratitude to you, infinite being, for joining me on this journey and allowing me to be your guide.

I see you.

I feel you.

I hear you.

I know you.

I love you.

I have so much gratitude from my heart, for connecting me with yours, and I would like to congratulate you on making it this far. Your journey has only just begun.

My desire is that some part of this book has been a useful resource to help you navigate your spiritual awakening and has provided a soothing balm for your body-temple, mind-temple, and heart-temple. I know your soul knows the way and needs no soothing; it is pure unconditional love, connected to source energy and will provide you all the innate wisdom, love, and guidance you will need through your human experience. I am connected to you in Oneness.

We are only beginning to peel back the many layers of conditioning, no matter what stage of your life you are at. There is always more to un-learn and more to re-member.

You have awakened all that is possible within yourself. You have opened up to new potentiality, new paradigms, and reconnected with your innate power and wisdom. Spirituality is the unfolding of your soul and embodiment is intrinsic to your new way of being.

There are many stages to our spiritual awakening, to remembering who we truly are, our power, our potential, and our soul gifts.

Knowing that "knowledge isn't power, applied knowledge is power" – all that we now know and have unpacked during our time together, it is imperative to embody your new higher-habits and reclaim God-self.

Integration is a crucial step towards living your life with purpose and passion. Your soul is always calling you to reveal your dharma, your sacred truth to the world. I believe it is imperative you follow this call. To not do so would diminish your brilliant light and create chaos in your life.

Revisit the Life Structure Review that you completed in #3: Soul Alignment. Measure your results from day one when you first began this journey until now. This will help give you a tangible reflection in your results of your growth. I believe if you applied all the lessons in this handbook, completed all the *SacredPlay*, you will have grown, awakened to greater potential and received greater insights to the unfolding of your soul.

There is always more to experience, more to expand, more to unfold. This is what makes life truly exciting.

If we are not growing, we are dying. The Universe is constantly expanding and it is imperative we do the same. We are infinite spiritual beings of the Universe; we are required to grow and why wouldn't we? There is so much this Earthly human experience has to offer. It is our duty to partake, to be a full and willing participant in our life.

Life is about pleasure, not pain. It is only our conditioning that makes us believe otherwise. Remind yourself of your power daily, take time for pleasure daily – whatever that looks like for you. It may be sitting mindfully, sipping tea in the morning. It could be meditating daily on your vision and goals. Whatever pleasure is for you, take time every day to embrace this magnificent life.

Reflect on any moments of insight you have experienced during this journey. What "aha" moments have you received? What light-bulb moments have occurred? Write these in the space below. The process of self-reflection continues as your consciousness and awareness rises.

If you allow yourself to expand in ways you never believed possible, your perception shifts; new doorways will open for you; your reality changes as you begin creating your own destiny.

Listen to your heart. Take note of what is in your head. Listen to the subtle whispers of your body and pay attention to your soul's calling. Your innate wisdom and guidance will deliver you to a life filled with self-empowerment and self-love.

You may wish to revisit this handbook from time to time and find that each time you do so, you will gain new knowledge and insights. As your consciousness grows, so does your level of receptivity, understanding, and integration.

Your success is inevitable. You are already all the things you desire, now to just get out of your own way. I believe it to be true and I believe in you.

It is done.

It is done.

It is done.

By the power of three, the holy trinity, it is done. May this holy trinity that you are forever connected with be that of your human being, spiritual being, and the Universe or God-source.

All the very best, my dear friends. May you continue to grow and flourish in this Earthly realm, thrive in your human experience, and truly LIVE. Until we meet again.

With love and gratitude,

Aida Jasmine

Find Your Way Home

My purpose is to awaken you to yours. With this intention, I ask that for the empowerment of this Divine Mother Earth, all planets, the Universe, animals, and other human beings to please help get this message out to awaken others to their own brilliance and potential.

Please like, share, and subscribe to all media to help spread the word.

You may also connect with me through my email, website, or social media and join our family and community.

Website:
aidajasmine.org

You are Love.

You are Loving.

You are Loved.

You are Loveable.

So it is.

It is done.

For the good of all, harm to none.

A'ho.

Gratitude

It is with deep heart-felt, soul-filled gratitude that I wish to give a prayer of acknowledgement to the original custodians of this land. I wish to pay my respect to all Elders past, present, and emerging. I thank you for the care and protection of this sacred land. May you be blessed and honoured. May we join together and build a future based on compassion, love, hope, faith, and reconciliation.

I wish to pay homage and give deep reverence to this Divine Mother Earth, this sacred Earth who continues to give, no matter how much we take. She is a Divine representation of compassion and unconditional love.

I wish to thank all the beautiful beings who have joined me on my journey through this Earthly experience so far. You have all impacted my life in many ways that has led me to have certain experiences and write this book. For that, I am truly grateful.

My beloved Mumma, I love you; I remember you; I thank you. All that I am is because of you. Our sacred soul contract enabled us to dance through this life and many others, and for that, I am truly grateful. You taught me how to live through life with poise, grace, ease, flow, and beauty. You showed me unconditional love beyond mother and daughter; it was a higher level of love, one that is truly celestial that we called

Agapé. You showed me that wherever one places their faith, you will find your strength. You always reminded me to come back home to my power, my strength, and to take no shit. Your ability to instantly manifest in the physical reality was awe-inspiring. Your gifts of beauty and talent live with me, and I will forever miss your song. I love you ever so deeply.

My beloved Baron. You taught me unconditional love, unwavering loyalty, that strength comes from within and even the small are oh, so mighty. You reminded me of my determination, fearlessness, vulnerability, and steadfastness – that no matter how many times my heart breaks, it is breaking open. Forever by my side, always in my heart. Deep love and gratitude for you.

Dear Dad, thank you. You showed me my strength, how resilient I can be and that what doesn't kill me makes me stronger. Thank you for agreeing to be a part of this life and for our journey together. Knowing that everything happens exactly as it 'should', as it is meant to play out, that everything is part of a Divine plan, timing, and order. I believe we choose our experiences, soul, and spirit team before we come down to Earth to play. From that higher realm, I graciously and gratefully accept these roles and express deep gratitude for you. I love you.

I feel truly blessed and grateful for all the experiences and lessons I have learned in this lifetime and for the many people who have showed up in my life.

For all my students, anyone's life who has touched mine on this journey, you taught me to be a better teacher, guide, and mentor – thank you; I love you.

To all who made this body of work possible and creating this book into physical reality, my publisher, cover designer, editors, and proofreaders, thank you.

For my Spirit team and all celestial beings, thank you for your continued guidance and support, deep heart-felt, soul-filled gratitude, without which this book would not have been brought to life. Deep gratitude for allowing me to be a conduit for the Divine and trusting me with sharing these messages with humanity.

To the infinite Oneness, Source Energy, I am home. I am Love.

Thank you All, I am truly grateful. I love you.

I know there are many more experiences to embrace, more to learn and more to unfold. I am excited for the next chapter and adventure of my life.

Until we meet again.

Deep love and gratitude,

Aida Jasmine

About Aida Jasmine

Aida Jasmine is a Magick weaver, Witch, Divine Feminine Embodiment mentor and Ascension Mastery Guide who empowers women around the world to unleash their fullest potential. She is a wayshower, mapmaker, guide, teacher, mentor, and healer. She doesn't tell you what to see, rather, where to look: within.

Aida is a spiritual activator and loves to ignite people to uncover their dharma, unique soul expression, and live with purpose whilst experiencing life on Mumma Earth. Her purpose is to remind you of your innate power, wisdom, and the powerful infinite being that you are by reconnecting with yourself and living a purpose-filled, blissful, abundant life.

Aida calls herself Witch: a woman in her power, the Divine feminine flow that is in alignment with Mother Nature, Earth. Living this truth is what led her to unravel the mysteries of the Divine and unlock codes for living abundantly on this Earth. She runs a Mystery School, sharing this wisdom with others to unlock their true potential and create Heaven on Earth.

At a very early age, Aida tapped into her spiritual gifts. She is a generational Witch, Spirit and Psychic Medium, and Healer, spending the greater part of her life learning, un-learning, deep-diving, and harnessing her skills to be of service to others.

Aida weaves all her magick into her work. You will feel her gentle strength and power and leave her presence feeling seen, heard, safe, and expanded.

All of you is welcome in Aida's temple and Mystery School. To connect with her visit...

www.aidajasmine.org

www.ingramcontent.com/pod-product-compliance
Ingram Content Group UK Ltd.
Pitfield, Milton Keynes, MK11 3LW, UK
UKHW061223180426
11947UKWH00027B/1993